Portrait
of an
Innocent

Ivan Cañadas Fraile

Copyright © Ivan Cañadas 2021
Email: artsonasoc@yahoo.com

Photographs by Maria Pilar Fraile Perea.

Cover design by Rica Cabrex.

Cañadas Fraile, Ivan.
        Portrait of an Innocent / Ivan Cañadas Fraile.

ISBN-13: 9780645113501 (Paperback)
ISBN-13: 9780645113518 (Epub)

This book is dedicated with my deepest
gratitude to my parents, Luis Cañadas Benítez
and María Pilar Fraile Perea.

Contents

Preschool.

I'm five. The nuns have taken to sitting around after their late-morning meal of soup and bread-and-cheese while I read them the newspaper.

Later, I'm out in the playground, too grown-up now for the sandpit, I become Tarzan, King of the Jungle. Beating my chest rhythmically, *rat-tat-tat*, I make the jungle-cry, and then leap onto the monkey bars. My arms stretch, long and thin, like Saturday-morning spaghetti. I swing lazily from bar to bar.

Tired of that, as the sun beats down on the gray schoolyard, I adopt my uncle's cool-guy amble, past a little girl on all fours. I stop dead in my tracks, disgusted to see her crawling like that—like a baby. She must be two-and-a-half.

She has her two hands on the cement. Her fingers stretch out like tentacles—like snails peeping from their shell. Transfixed, I watch them move over the hot ground, cracks peopled with busy ants, large and fleshy. The silly girl cannot even walk. Tensing, I look around, as a familiar chant drones in my ears:

Don't kill the wee-little ants, for they were made by God.
Don't kill...

I tread on her hand with my brand-new sneakers. Twice because, at first, she doesn't even cry out. She just looks at me, her eyes growing large. Then, she lets out an unearthly shriek, scarier than Tarzan, and I run for it because I think one of the nuns has shouted my name. Inside, I crouch behind one of the desks. Nobody saw me...

Mum comes to pick me up after her workday's done. There's the shouting and laughter of children reunited with their parents. At the portal, I bury my head in her waist.

"I'm going to cut your hands off", the voice seethes with anger. The woman could be of my aunts in the country. Large and red-faced, she has short hair and powerful arms. She towers over Mum, who turns with a gasp and asks in a strange, high-pitched voice:

"What are you saying to my son?"

"I'm going to cut off your hands!" She directs this at me, ignoring Mum. I stare in confusion. The little girl is not on the ground now. She stands behind the woman, but is also frowning with something of her mother's indignation.

"He stepped on her hands—there, where you see him with his good-boy face", the lady explains to my mother, who retorts automatically:

"No, that's impossible. He wouldn't..." Pausing, with a sudden look of disbelief, Mum turns to me.

"It's impossible", I echo. I look at the little girl, dumbfounded: "I ... I ..."

"She told me *everything*", says the lady, gesturing toward her daughter as the veracity of the claims now sink in my mother's mind, who stares at me is disbelief while I, unable to meet her gaze, and still barely able to comprehend, blurt out:

"But, she couldn't do anything.... How...?"

"She told me", the lady repeats with a hint of pride in her voice. The girl, though quiet still, one hand on her mother's skirted waist, looks at me directly.

It's now the next morning, and my parents will never forgive me again. Last night, Dad said that he refused to bring up a fascist in his house—he'd send me to reform school first—and that he had never wanted me to go to the nuns in the first place.

Mum defended me. But, then, she cried: "Why would he hurt a little girl like that?" Now, I listen outside their room, breathing softly, so they won't hear me.

When I try to kiss him good morning in the big bed, Dad says: "Oh, no… no more." Mum, too, looks away, her face pale, drawn. I hang my head in shame and weep silently, big tears rolling down my cheeks. They will never love me anymore. A little later, softened, they both hug me firmly, and tell me to promise that I will never do anything like that again.

El practicante.

I'm with Mum, who is walking very slowly today. Now and then, she stops and breathes out heavily, like *Escubi*, Grandad's smooth black dog with the deep, sad eyes and floppy ears, who lets you play with them. Escubi never bites because Grandad doesn't let the silly children throw stones. Because dogs don't know, so they fetch rocks with their toothy mouths. But you should only throw sticks. Not like Mum's favorite dog, which was very nice until other people played pranks like that and made it turn mean. He wasn't really bad, really. But his teeth hurt a lot, so he wanted to bite the stupid children.

We go to the shop to get bread and milk and many things. But today, we are going to another place. This is not our house. The door is large and black, and we go in and Mum holds my hand and stops, breathing heavily, to pat my head. I like to pat Escubi's head, but I cannot see him now because he's at Grandad's house, running faster than the rabbits and chasing the magpies and the crows, so they won't eat Grandad's grapes. But I want to see him soon.

Mum takes me by the hand because we have to go up the stairs for a long, long time. We stop many times. Mum says that she has to get her breath back, and I breathe like Escubi, too, with my tongue hanging out, and Mum laughs softly, and holds her belly. She tells me to stop that because laughing hurts. But laughing is funny. It doesn't hurt.

She lets go of my hand because she says that we are there already. She takes a paper out from her bag and pushes the button on the door that rings like the telephone. And there is a funny picture on the door. The man has a smile and a white jacket, and I remember this door…

And, again, I hear the doorbell go *riiiiiinggg* while Mum says: "Don't tell me, after this long walk that the *practicante* is not going to be here!"

But, I'm already rushing down the stairs. I'll go home, and Dad will say that I don't have to come here anymore. And Grandad will find me and I'll play with Escubi in his house and eat cheese and little grapes that Grandma hangs from the ceiling and gave me last time. And Mum yells out behind me and tells me to wait, and I can hear her big feet, as she runs after  me and she breathes through her mouth. I turn quickly around and I think that I will fall. But I don't fall and I run down again and I run straight. But there's a door. And then, Mum is behind me, and she puts her arms around me, hugs me tight, and tells me not to be afraid.

*   *   *

One of my earliest memories is of a course of injections I received when I was probably not quite two. Rightly or wrongly, I retain the distinct impression that doctors in my early childhood were fond of prescribing injections—courses of five or six shots, for the merest common cold. It may have been that patients themselves, brought up when vaccination campaigns were standard, actually expected that sort of thing. Parents, grandparents, friends, neighbors—*anybody*—leaving a doctor's office in the '70s felt somehow neglected if they weren't issued a prescription for some ampoules.

"What did Dr. López give you?" one neighbor asks another.

"Oh, nothing, at all. Just some capsules. He tells me to drink lots of water, get some bed-rest, and eat lots of fruit and vegetables. He must think that I'm a rabbit, or something!'

"It serves you right! You should have gone to Dr. Jiménez, like I told you. I went there, yesterday—because, you know I had a bit of a sore shoulder, all the way up the neck when I got up, yesterday?"

"Uh-huh…"

"Well, good Dr. Jiménez … *he* listens to you when you drop by, *not like some others*… It turns out it was a spot of the flu—very bad stuff, this year. But, luckily we've caught it in time and nipped it in the bud."

"He's prescribed you some injections, then?"

"But of course! Say what we will, there's nothing like it…"

But, this prescription would have been useless without the all-important *practicante*, a kind of nurse or paramedic, whose job was to give you the prescribed *pinchazos*—the shots. Some carried the telltale briefcase or satchel from house to house. Others you'd have to visit yourself. Either way, their role was to inject the contents of those little ampoules from the pharmacy into your freshly-swabbed butt-cheek.

This was a recurring ritual, coinciding with the arrival of every winter and the first sign of a cold. No dentist ever saw the inside of my mouth prior to my eighteenth birthday, but I definitely remember the *practicantes* of my childhood. In the cultural imaginary of those years, these were among every child's bogeymen—or *women*—of our everyday, no matter how adept members of this profession usually were at helping kids to relax before the jab. I'm certain that a good bedside manner was as important in their profession as it is for any other nurse or doctor.

"I see. So, have you started getting your shots?" one neighbor asks another.

"Of course—you've just caught me on the way to see Alfonso— the new *practicante*."

"Ahhhh… is that the tall, good-looking one that I've heard so much about?", asks Neighbor One with a knowing twinkle in her eye.

"I don't know that he's as tall as all that. But, as for being *majo*… ummh … yes. When he looks at you, you don't even feel the needle."

"I *see*…"

"No", she coughs. "You *don't*. But, anyway, I should run. It's not right to be late when you have an appointment with the *practicante*."

*   *   *

I also remember visiting a doctor, whose practice was always warm, like his smile and his soft voice. He'd check your neck, just in case it was your tonsils, and he'd ask polite questions of Mum, who obviously placed great trust upon him. Not surprisingly, I spent several years determined that, one day, I, too, would be a doctor. I'd save lives and take care of children and of their Mums. A doctor, I'd explain—my nervousness and speed often mistaken for a stutter— and not just any ordinary, lazy one, who didn't know anything, but "*uno de los buenos-buenos!*"

I committed my first act of infidelity the day I allowed a friend of the family—a man who worked as a mechanic for Iberia—to talk me into abhorring medicine and doctors and the blood and guts that, oddly enough, no-one had warned me about. Watched by my parents, their knowing smiles barely concealed, this man—as engaging in his own way as the proverbial barber-surgeon—told me exciting stuff about aircraft and of the airline's elite, the pilots who flew those giants of the sky, and who led exciting lives, travelling and enjoying free holidays, caviar, Champagne and beautiful girls wherever they went!

Abandoning my first intended calling with only a twinge of guilt, I immediately decided that I would become an airline pilot. I would travel all round the world, earn lots of my money in my clean shirt and tie and be attended by pretty stewardesses with long hair and even longer legs. So I told everyone I met.

Doctors, nurses and *practicantes*… long before they were betrayed for the fantastic life of an airline pilot—and, even before they were respected and admired—had been merely dreaded. My respect for these strange people in white jackets and the cold things that they pressed to your back and chest, who made you feel better when you were sick—and who jabbed your bum if so required—had started one day, not too long after our visit to the *practicante*. It was the day when the doctors helped Mum and Dad to bring home my baby brother.

The Boots

D ad would go on his rounds, drumming up new clients for the insurance company. Later, he'd deal with the paperwork. He was an accountant, as the diploma on the wall of his study declared. Work was particularly heavy one week a month, the one devoted not to finding new clients but to collecting the monthly premiums from existing ones. For this task, Dad would strap on a leather pouch to his waist, and, for days, he'd climb up and down the stairs of apartment buildings. He'd joke about how his weight regularly went up and down due to that fourth week each month.

But, when I was really small, I saw another side of his work. This was on Saturdays when the agents would submit completed paperwork at the head office before gathering at a nearby bar to knock back a beer or two, talk about work or their families, tell a couple of jokes and have something to eat together. I remember going sometime when Luis and I we were already in primary school. But, I also remember accompanying Dad to the head office around the time when I was almost two and Luis was born.

It's also the boots that I remember: lace-up hiking boots for little kids, which were beautiful and probably cost my parents an arm and a leg—or a *kidney*, as we often say in Spain. Frugal about most things, my parents refused to skimp when it came to the food on the table, our education or our clothes. Dad was proud of his prattling parrot of a son. I, in turn, wanted to show everyone my boots—first, at the office, and, later, at the bar.

I remember my father as a very busy man whom we'd await longingly—Mum and I and, later, Luis, too. He might arrive late from a meeting when Luis and I were already supposed to be asleep. But, he'd tiptoe into our room to kiss us goodnight, anyhow, guessing rightly that he'd find us awake. I remember how he sat me up, once to give me an apricot-flavored sweet— which he unwrapped and put into my mouth, as he kissed my forehead. Behind him, Mum whispered urgently: "It's  very late, and he's already cleaned his teeth...."

"Just because of one time, he's not going to get cavities," Dad said.

But the story of the boots is one of my earliest memories. I loved those things so much—their tough, sturdy design and thick soles, and the laces that bound them firmly to feet and ankles. I stood, feeling proud, wanting everyone to admire them. The day I was given them, I wore them to sleep, refusing to take them off. A true mountaineer, I clambered over the wooden railing of my crib. Only once I was sound asleep—booted feet asunder, one clenched fist above my head in a no-doubt reassuring gesture—was Mum able to loosen the laces and remove the boots, so that I was surprised to find them on the floor, by my crib, the following morning.

The crib, incidentally, would not be mine for much longer. It would go to Luis, the baby, who had been growing inside Mum's belly.

I remember being *so* excited when he was finally brought home: "*¡El bebé, el bebé!*" I think that I expected a little creature, like Garbancito or Pulgarcito—the Chickpea/Tom Thumb character. Instead, there was my baby brother, bursting with health and larger-than-life, just shy of ten pounds.

At home, I was temporarily moved to a spare bed until a new child's bed could be bought. A few minutes, later, annoyed that I'd been driven from my own crib, which now boasted pride of place in my parents' room, I stalked the length of the corridor—elbows out by my sides, a frown that tugged at my forehead and the heavy tread that I'd learnt from wearing my big boots.

I climbed over the railing and finding that the baby was taking up the center of the crib in blissful slumber, I lay down on top of him and promptly went to sleep. Mum, as she later revealed, saw me come in, a child on a mission. She said nothing. Having worked as a nanny from the age of fourteen until she married seven years or so later, she had seen the green eyes of sibling rivalry up close. So, she gave me a minute to doze off, and, then, carefully fished out the new bundle of joy.

Luis slept in their bed that night. But I had no idea about that when I woke up in the morning. I remembered where I was with satisfaction before I realized that—like my boots—the baby had banished! I gasped, thinking that I had squashed him flat. I sat up with a start and recoiled to the edge of the crib.

"He's right here," Mum said, gesturing to her side. "Don't worry."

I was very relieved to see that the baby was sleeping placidly. Mum, then, sat me up with her, and, whispering softly lest he wake, explained, *in confidence*, that he was very small and needed us to take care of him. From that moment, I looked at him differently—and I never tried to reclaim the crib again.

Questions

Luis and I are very small, dressed in what look like matching painter's smocks, the school uniform that we wore in kindergarten. Mum is taking us home, and it's very nice out. On our away across a field, we pass a persimmon tree, and Mum warns me not to rub against some low-hanging fruit, overripe and dripping. The orange pulp leaves a stain that's very hard to remove. I wonder, is that why they call it a *caqui?*

Building workers—loud men, perched tens of meters above the ground—are forever on the lookout for young women to shower with extravagant compliments, catcalls, wolf-whistles. Embarrassment is met with laughter and with renewed efforts to get a rise out of the women. Some women respond salaciously with humor of their own while others are offended and respond with abuse. Both probably make the workers' day.

I have heard Mum criticize some women for the way they react. They get offended by some off-color call, or at very idea of being propositioned or talked about in that fashion, so they swear at the men, call them *maricones*, or *machistas de mierda*. They stand in the street, staring at the sky above telling the voices there to go and get fucked, drawing attention to themselves.

We have heard some of their strange compliments, delivered in tear-throat, teasing tones. They call her a little girl "*¡Nehhhhh-*

naaaaaaaaaa! ¡Chi-qui-llaaaaaaaaaa!" They'll ask her, in the same tone, if *all that* is hers. Mum never huddles in response; if anything, she holds her head higher. They whistle and laugh. Mum usually ignores them—just hustles Luis and me along, and tells us to pay no attention. But, I cannot help looking back, squinting into the sunlight, trying to make out the shouters high up in the scaffolding. Mum drags me along: "Don't pay any attention. If not, it's worse!"

I can sort-of understand that they think she's pretty. People are often surprised that she's our Mum. They think that she is our big sister. Part of me is proud of the way that she turns heads. But Luis, though younger than I, catches on that they have somehow offended our Mum. So, he squares up to them, clenched fists down by his sides. Enraged that they are so far away, and growing red in the face because he cannot hit them, he shouts at them, instead—calls them idiots, and, his latest word, *jilipollas* (dickheads). He can get so mad, though barely three. The men up in the building site are crestfallen, ashamed. "Sorry, kid! We didn't mean any harm. Don't cry."

"*Chaval ... machote*", they call him. It is true. He is a brave little kid—assertive, manly in a sense, though a bit bad-tempered.

"*A ver... tch, tch, tch! Si es que, ¡no hay derecho!*" A woman going by joins us on the footpath, sympathizes with Mum, and pats Luis's head. It is not right, she says, a disgrace.

Mum puts her arms around him, lifts him up. *Nothing's happened. Nothing's wrong, darling. Come on, let's go.* We move on, as a couple of the workers apologize, Mum brushing it aside with a sweep of her hand, wanting no more of it. She leads us away, both on foot, now.

But, before we get home, a well-dressed older woman—posh-looking, with jewelry and a haughty, commanding tone—accosts Mum. More to herself than to us, but nonetheless expecting a response, she declares: "Why, these children must be Miro's!"

"Sorry—what's that you're saying?" My mother is caught unawares, sounds disconcerted. She looks quizzically at the lady.

"These children", the lady enunciates clearly and firmly, as she raises my chin with thumb and forefinger to peer at my profile; she lets the words hang in the air, then adds, something like impatience creeping in:

"They *are* Miró's?"

"No…" Mum frowns, now, enough time for her own character to kick into gear. "They are *mine!*"

"Yes, of course they *are*! But are they Miró's?"

"No! They are my husband's! I don't know any Miró."

"Oh, there's no reason to get snappy. They *are* the spitting image of Miró!"

Mum has had enough; shrugging, she adds, a little irritated: "I've already told you", as we push onwards along the street, eager to get home.

The Valencian *huerta*

For several decades, the Valencian *huerta*—the market gardens supported by *acequias*, a network of irrigation channels and ditches dating back to the region's Moorish period, have shrunk at an abysmal pace before progress. Apartment buildings, freeways and shopping malls gobbled up some of the most fertile acres in the country. Some forty years ago, however, it was still possible to live in a place like Alboraya. Though the town had already been engulfed by the suburbs of Valencia, it still retained many of those ancient plots of land. So, people lived in new apartment buildings overlooking a veritable oasis. There, across the street from our own apartment, there was one such family of *hortelanos*. The last of a line of proud tenant farmers, their lease kept in the family for generations, they had yet to give up their ancestral rights for some cash and a couple of apartments.

It was such farmers as these who would settle disputes over the use and abuse of communally-shared ditchwater at the *tribunal de las aguas*. There, each side was allowed their say through a simple but punitively enforced utterance of *calle vosté* and *parle vosté*, "you, quiet; you, speak."

From our fifth-floor perch, the apartment's balcony, we would gaze longingly at the expanse of greenery across the street. These were prosperous times. At the greengrocer's downstairs, we bought the lettuce or cabbage that he himself, in his farmer's hat, had picked that same morning, and there was always some chit-chat, and some kind words, a question about friends or family. It was hard to believe that we would be in a world of trouble if we were to, say, wander onto those lands; hard to believe that these were the same tough peasants who were reputed to guard their lands with fierce, wolfish dogs, their tails and ears cut off—the proverbial *perro del hortelano*, which "will not eat the greens, but won't let you, either"—and, in harder times, maybe even a trusty old shotgun, possibly also passed down through the generations—and loaded with rock salt *if* the *hortelano* was kindly, some tellers added for effect with a sideways wink at our parents. However much such tales may have stretched the truth, I never tired of hearing them as a child.

Of course, there were stories of other times—of the fearsome post-war period during which many Spaniards, particularly those who were deprived of a parent by the prison camp or the firing squad, had suffered grievous poverty and deprivation. This period was poignantly referred to as *los años del hambre*, "the famine years."

Though, at first, they might seem irredeemably grim, such stories were defiant affirmations of survival, inherent in the very fact that they were being retold. Here, after all, was the narrator, transformed into a hero. In fact, no matter who did the telling, or what they were like the rest of the time, this hero tended to be a bit of a character. Naturally, the theme of hunger prompted stories of times when they had gone some way to overcome it. Whether they were successful or not was another matter...

As the richest vegetable plot in Spain, along with Murcia, Valencia surely offered the down-and-outs the best pickings. It would be fair to say that this place was relatively spared the worst of the famine. But, there were certainly stories of unauthorized fruit-picking, of the vengeful-rueful gobbling of the poor when they had a chance, and of mad dashes across moonlit fields—the snapping jaws of Cerberus behind a hungry kid's backside—ending in a blind leap over an *acequia* to safety. Even a bad fall or a beating—rough justice from an outraged farmer or shopkeeper—or the concerned severity of parents, fearful of what would happen if their son were caught, seemed a small price for the triumph of telling such a tale.

Only one thing was sacrosanct in Valencia: the artichokes, so good that I have never tasted their like anywhere else. As our local friends explained, artichokes must be picked in a particular order. Pick one of the medium ones, rather than the largest one, and the smaller ones would not grow. Imagine the unwitting damage that a thief could cause, hastily filling a sack in the dark, like a two-legged goat. No possible humor in that, no sympathy.

Closer to my own time, I remember the story of an older friend of the family—thirteen or fourteen? I'm not sure—but obviously old enough to set out with some friends and cousins on a rough-and-ready camping trip. They were supposed to go as far as El Saler, a park ringed with pine trees, near La Albufera, the lagoon and wetlands formed by the delta of the local Turia river. Soon tired of walking, and weighed down with backpacks and camping equipment in the summer heat, they only got as far as a plot of land lying fallow, not too far from the neighborhood of Benimàmet, where they lived.

It was then, as night fell, that they realized that in all their excitement they had not packed any food. However, there was a *huerta* nearby, and after a couple of hours of ignoring the gnawing in their bellies—and raised hearing tales of outwitting the landholder, they decided to raid the plot.

True, there was nothing particularly appetizing growing there. No persimmons or oranges—in fact, not even tomatoes and lettuces. But, as they felt famished, the green beans and half-grown cabbages there would do just fine. It also didn't occur to them, prior to wolfing down those freshly picked vegetables, that maybe they should wash off the pesticides.

Later that night, they returned home crying, their faces half-swollen with an alarming rash—something between a welt and a blister, so I was told. And so, they trekked straight into a cold bath, calamine lotion and the universal laughter of every adult in the whole

wine-guzzling, all-singing, all-dancing neighborhood, who were in the midst of a street party, fathers, uncles, older brothers, already rather warm with wine, women and song.

As the domestic setting of many childhood memories, an apartment overlooking the centuries-old acreage, I still feel attached to the place, much as I know that it is no longer there. Memories, however, are contradictory things—insubstantial and subject to distortion, yet, paradoxically, the only thing that may survive the pace of progress, which raises and as readily bulldozes with utter disdain those structures and localities that our ancestors held sacred. But, in such a world, all that is left is memory.

One of mine is of my younger brother, four or five and known for the most amazing tantrums—something primeval. I like to think that these developed into his subsequent patience and determination.

He had a way of looking straight at you with the biggest frown. If annoyed further, the telltale vein on the side of his neck would stick out, and, *then*, you knew he was really pissed off. Even in his sleep—while I dreamt of world domination, or of the two Yolandas in my class—Luis would rave against some kid or other who annoyed him at school. Mum and Dad chuckled at the breakfast table—about the extent of the child's precocious collection of expletives, discovered when they had walked into our bedroom in response to a particularly loud dream the night before. When they saw our faces light up, however, they suddenly looked stern; *we were not to say things like that*. In fact, we were probably lucky that our parents were not the kind to wash a child's mouth out with soap and water.

Not wanting to drink his milk—the same milk that Luis would cry and sulk about if he didn't get it fast enough—sometimes triggered a full-blown tantrum. Luckily, Mum had mastered the art of reverse psychology.

"Whatever you like. Leave the milk there. A dog will come and drink it, as soon as you walk away."

Shaken by the prospect of losing his milk, which he loved to drink, after all, he guzzled it down.

In a now-legendary blowout, he raced out of the kitchen with one of Mum's earthenware pots, which he proceeded to hurl out the window with a yell: "*¡A la acequia!*" But, of course, it did not make it to the irrigation ditch across the street. Rather, it smashed on the pavement five floors below. Maybe we needed to get out more.

Some of this stubbornness grew into… patience, I suppose. True, we found various things to keep ourselves entertained. It was easy for me: I read. Sometimes, I'd draw something on our blackboard, or I'd try out some crayons. But, for the most part, I read. He was different. When Mum started working at the Polytechnic University, she would bring us lots of discarded assignment papers from the architecture students, as well as pencils, drawing paper and other expensive items that spoilt students often simply abandoned in the exam rooms at the end of their courses. Enthralled, he would sit for hours, pencil, eraser and compass in hand, carefully copying technical drawings, and, when he was done, we often couldn't tell which one was the original and which one the copy.

We spent a lot of time inside, the street below being a little dangerous for kids our age; mad traffic aside, there were the would-be street thugs, talk of a drug epidemic, and faceless vandals, like the ones who set fire to one of our car tires; besides, one of the neighborhood women had been held up in the elevator, a knife to her throat, just for a little grocery money.

So, we spent most of our time inside, five floors above the concrete jungle, shielded by a protective barrier of wooden blocks; barricaded behind books; wrapped in a six-year-old's architectural drawings.

Other times, of course, we were a bit more active. We were forbidden to play ball in the apartment; there were neighbors to consider. But whenever Mum dashed to the shop downstairs for some milk or whatever, out came the ball, which we kicked all over the place, bounced it off the walls…

One particular day, a figurine tumbled down off the shelf and smashed on the floor. *Oh, no! We're in for it now*, we thought. Unless we did something, we'd face every child's fear—the dreaded slipper was sure to come off!

Well, not necessarily. There's always superglue. I quickly fetched it. But, as I gazed hopelessly at the pile of fragments sitting on the table, I heard a voice, calm and firm: "Why don't you let me do that?"

Perhaps, my own general clumsiness had already been revealed. Whatever the reason, Luis proceeded to stick the figurine together again, and it went back on the shelf looking as good as new—*almost*.

And so, a couple of months went by. Mum would pick up that figurine, at least once a week, as she dusted everything, and, more often than not, I would be right there watching her, trying to look innocent, trying to look away, biding my time—*Oooh, she's going to notice...*

But, one day, of course, she did notice a little hairline fracture, and examining the figurine more carefully, she realized that it was not just the one little crack. In fact, it had been smashed to smithereens and stuck together again. Had she not noticed at the store, she pondered?

Mum, of course, confronted the one who didn't know how to keep a secret to save his life: *me*. So, Mum did get to the bottom of it, after all. But, by then, she couldn't get angry, anymore.

La Casa de Campo:
June 1977

L *a Casa de Campo*: the old hunting grounds of Spanish royalty. On the first of May, 1931, in one of the first acts of the Second Spanish Republic, the land, ceded to the people of Madrid, became the community's largest public park. About 1700 hectares in size, it is five times larger than New York's Central Park, and seventeen times larger than Sydney's Olympic Park.

In June 1977, when I was five, this was the site of one of the most memorable mass gatherings to take place in the years of my childhood. It was the first of the Communist Party's annual festivals, and the largest—attracting a million people from all over the country, only weeks after the party's legalization in April. Earlier that year, on the 24th of January, a gang of right-wing *ultras* had raided a legal support office in Atocha, Madrid, where they sprayed bullets, wounding several and killing five, among them labor lawyers and other activists. As is often the case with the actions of extremists, it backfired. Widespread disgust at the actions of the assassins led to a nationwide strike, while the funeral of the trade unionists was attended by 100,000 people, in the first mass-demonstration by the Left since the death of Franco.

The scandal, in fact, had sped up the legalization of the PCE, Spain's communist party. For many, and not only those who belonged to the party, it was the final confirmation that democracy had arrived: the day in which even the ideological archenemies of the fascists were finally back in the democratic fold. Concessions were made by all sides, of course. The following year, in accordance with the processes of *desovietización*, the PCE would style itself *"Marxista, revolucionario y democrático."*

I'm sure that there were speeches beyond my understanding, though I do remember sing-alongs, and chants of *"¡El pueblo unido jamás será vencido!"* in an atmosphere of joy and excitement, and everywhere the food stalls, loud music and people cheering and singing of any fairground. I remember a Chilean band playing a song, whose chorus referred to a black eagle, destined to fall, and which people observed was about the rapacious American military. But, the camaraderie of the time and place was also the simple joviality of any other festival. I met a boy called Miguel with whom I played all day—in the sandpit, on the swings. We swore eternal friendship. I was amazed that we had the same taste in cartoons. My parents chuckled later. Yeah, like we're going to come all the way here, so you can play with your new friend. It hadn't occurred to me all day that I'd never see him again.

Today, militants look back on those days with nostalgia; for the annual festival—like membership in the Party—has long been but a shadow of what it once was. One commentator provided a poignant image of this decline in the person of the famous director, Juan Antonio Bardem—uncle of actor Javier—who sang the *Internationale* at the 2002 festival. The director's example was both moving and sad, since he was borne onto the stage in a stretcher, having only a month left to live.

* * *

We'd been lent a larger car, in exchange for our small Citroën. The other family wanted to take it out and roll back the convertible's canvas top. But, ironically, theirs broke down during the return trip. We were not far along that road from a small village, but it was very late at night and it was raining, the car's beams lighting up water drops into an incandescent blind.

Mum still felt that she was doing something wrong when the highway patrol came to our aid—*Guardia Civil* agents on motorcycles, no less—the car littered with P.C.E. and trade-union pamphlets, along with stickers that Luis and I had amassed in the course of the day, now plastered all over the windows. But, times *were* changing. The officers were nothing but courteous. They had our car towed to the nearest mechanic and contacted the manager of the village motel, so that a room would be ready in time for our arrival.

"But, they must have seen... They must have noticed," insisted Mum, still processing the new reality.

"Well, they are there to serve the public, after all," Dad responded, a note of pride in his voice betraying the fact that he understood perfectly well what she was getting at.

"Sure, but you know which leg those guys usually limp with."

"We have every right. *Ya ha llegado la libertad.*" Yes, freedom had finally arrived.

* * *

Things were changing, indeed. But, what we didn't know was that while we'd been attending that public manifestation of changing times, attended by a million people, an ultra-conservative clique was not sitting idly by.

This would culminate in two conspiracies, both of them involving the same officer of the police corps whose officers had treated us courteously that rainy night on a country road. Everyone in Spain, and many abroad, will recall at least some images of the seizure of parliament by two hundred machinegun-wielding civil guards in 1981. But, in some ways, more shocking is that Lt. Col. Antonio Tejero, who headed that foiled coup d'état, had already been apprehended before—only months after our attendance at that historical rally in 1977, in fact— when he had been caught in the act of putting together *Operación Galaxia*, a similar plot to overthrow the fledgling democratic government. More surprising still, to learn of it in Australia in 2007, as I sat at home with my father, on the thirtieth anniversary of the event; Spain's evening news were shown on SBS every morning, and Dad always made sure that they were recorded, so he could watch them after work. So, we gasped in unison, as Dad, too—politically active though he had been in those years—learned about how the judge, at the time, had given Tejero a sentence of only seven months, which had allowed the man, not even stripped of his membership or rank in the *Guardia Civil*, to make a far greater impression on the national psyche, four years later, on the notorious *23 de Febrero*, 1981.

Things were changing, indeed, but they would not do so immediately.

Mazinger-Zeta

I n the playground, we'd play around with the subject-matter of our daily existence, the culture that could only truly be our own once we'd messed with it.

The holy cows of yesteryear were fair game; even the national anthem was there to be parodied—to say nothing of Franco, "Protector of Spain by the Grace of God", as our coins still proclaimed. Bombarded as we also were with advertising campaigns for this-or-that laundry powder, certain to make your Mum the envy of all her neighbors, or commercials which trumpeted the latest thing in sanitary pads, or for *Ariel*-brand bleach—of which more below—it is hardly surprising that TV advertising should have contributed to the culture of the playground.

To the tune of the national anthem, we'd sing a ditty, which was, in fact, known the country over. It started like this:

Franco, Franco, tiene el culo blanco,
porque su mujer, se lo lava con Ariel...
(Franco, Franco, has a white behind, / Cos his wife uses Ariel till it shines.)

The man had died in 1975 when my classmates and I were three years old. So, by the time we were old enough to sing stuff like this, I'm sure that the *generalísimo's* lily-white backside was no more.

This was the end of the 1970s, going into the early '80s, and Japanese animation series were all the rage. Maybe hokey by today's standards, but, for us, at that moment in time, they were downright jaw-dropping.

Above them all, towered *Mazinger-Z* ("Mah-thing-guer-thetta", as we pronounced it). Mazinger—originally, *Majinga*, "the devil-god"—was an amazing robot, the product of a lost civilization, unearthed in a deserted island. Indestructible, and, thus, destined to be eternally victorious in battle, he had fortunately been found by the good guys. However, technology much like his own had fallen into the hands of the dastardly Baron Ashler, who was defeated each week, but would laugh demonically, as the credits rolled—promising more in the next episode.

By contrast, Mazinger-*Zeta* was Good. Although he triumphed every week—with a pandemonium of explosions, destruction and general mayhem—the opening theme song assured us that he was ever-ready to combat evil and always fought for peace. Mazinger was piloted by the heroes, who would race to get inside and shoot lasers at the enemy forces among sky scrapers, in cities deserted, as if magically deprived of their inhabitants by the neutron bomb. The exact nature of the latter, by the way, was actually a hot topic among seven- and eight-year-olds during the lunch-break at school.

Mazinger's strong points included a detachable head that functioned independently as a kind of fighter plane, and the red laser rays which shot out of his eyes. But, best of all, were his fists, which could be shot out missile-fashion, a heavyweight-fighter's dream-come-true, to the chant of "*puños fuera!*" ("fists out!"), echoed by millions of children, in lounge-rooms across the nation. *Mazinger-Z* must have really made an impression on people other than myself; suffice it to say that there's a ten-meter statue of him, *not* in Japan but in Tarragona, south-west of Barcelona.

With a start like this, I should have turned out to be a *manga* geek, in years to come, or, at least, an avid follower of the *Teenage Mutant Ninja Turtles* or *Transformers*. But, this never happened. Very soon, in fact, the whole genre simply struck me with an unbearable sense of nostalgia, not for that animation series, or for its dubious production values, but for the moment in childhood when it was possible to enjoy it all without irony.

Indeed, the wily worm of nostalgia began to devour the apple of childhood bliss almost before it was ripe. By the time *Com(m) ando-G*, another Japanese animation series that basked in the glow of *Star Wars*, it was old hat.

Our mothers, who came to pick us up from school and found us in a state of virtual hysteria were rather amused. A lot more than they had been with our recent spoof on *Mazinger*—so *last year* that we could poke fun at it, now. But, our teacher had been less than amused by what she called an obscene song, which she'd deemed serious enough to report to our parents:

Cuando sube la marea
Mazinger busca pelea;
puños fuera, rayos laser
y a la mierda el Baron Ashler.

("When the tide rises high / Mazinger looks for a fight / Fists come out, lasers hit / And Baron Ashler can go shit.")

Our mothers shrieked in unison, telling us to say to say the meaningless "*a la porra*", in place of the offending expression. Like most parents, they also would have preferred: *jolines* over *joder*—*freak*, not *fuck*; buzz off, not bugger off; gosh rather than God—whatever *gosh* means—and, so on. But, what would our friends think of us if we started to talk like that? The average parent wouldn't survive a week in elementary school!

In fact, I learnt much later that older children—and *not just* children—would sing much *harder* versions of this song, involving not only Mazinger, but also Sandokán—the swashbuckling protagonist of some Emilio Salgari novels, popularized in an Italian TV series of those years. The songs apparently alluded to sexual practices of which I hadn't even *heard*, so they went right over my innocent head.

Elementary School

It was the year I turned seven—at the start of second grade—that my elementary education began in earnest after a first year in which I had coasted, full of myself, on the reading and writing skills that the nuns—such as my first teacher, Sor Amalia—imparted upon their preschool charges. To kick off that second year, I spent the better part of three months sitting on a pile of sawdust, feet sticking out of the closet at the back of the classroom, where I read my way through the school's new collection of children's literature.

The teacher warned me that I should sit at my desk like everyone else and attend to the lessons, but she didn't press me when I shrugged and insisted that I'd rather read the books. I didn't think I had anything new to learn, my head a couple of sizes larger following the reading test at the end of the first year.

Inevitably, my hubris was duly punished when several of my classmates—some of whom had only learned to read during the previous year—bested me in the first-term examinations. Only then were my parents informed of my conduct in the preceding weeks. How they responded to the teacher's laissez-faire attitude I cannot honestly say. I do remember feeling ashamed and knowing that I only had myself to blame.

For all that, my mind was always wandering; my gaze would grow blank, and I would be unable to hear—to the point that people had to rouse me, as if from a dream. Seven, going eight, going nine, this was becoming something of a quirk. When not reading, my mind was a chamber, peopled with a multitude of characters, a private realm, enclosed yet all-encompassing, where vivid adventures, absorbing and often lurid, were projected. There, the prettiest girls offered themselves to me, even while I, the hero, guided my peers in a fierce resistance struggle.

One day, walking through a network of paths through the heart of the local *huerta*, on a school excursion to see seven medieval chapels, I was absorbed, willy-nilly, into a scenario in which terrorist-gangsters had taken the whole class-group hostage and shot the brave but ineffectual teacher, leaving any hope of rescue in the hands of the children.

At school, my nemesis, Victor—once, my best friend, as my parents invariably reminding me, but no longer so—darted across the roof, five floors up, yelling and drawing attention to himself. Admired or criticized, he was envied by every boy, especially when he had to report to the principal's office. He had stubbornly made his way to the top, his back to the wall, feet on the wall opposite in the narrow passageway that led to the square courtyard that the senior boys inexplicably called *el triangular*.

The long afternoons—the torrid siesta hours between 12:00 and 4:00 when most children went home before the late-afternoon session—I'd wander with a motley band of other boys from one playground to another and sometimes outside the school walls. Poorly supervised, we'd get up to all manner of mayhem.

When two years into school I was joined by my younger brother, who soon found his first girlfriend, the infantile lovebirds—adopted and celebrated by the uproarious older children—hugged and kissed inside an upended rubbish bin, which was, then, rolled and chased all over the playground by cheering, jeering children.

Another time, when *Fallas*-fever raged, I myself embarked on an errand. Tiny and rake-thin that I was, I squeezed between the bars on the front gate, off to buy firecrackers from the stall across the street, where the older boys could also buy their cigarettes by the unit.

Set on fire, the pile of balled-up test papers, cardboard, candy wrappers and plastic was as close as we schoolchildren would get to having a *falla* of our own. It burned fiercely, the rat-tat-tat of the tiny *chinos* followed by the loud boom of the red-and-blue-foiled *bombas*, which scattered ashes and half-burnt debris everywhere. Teachers ran outside to chide us while the playground filled with the beloved smell of black powder. An already hardening memento of molten black plastic would mark the ground for years to come.

Like every Valencian boy, a passion for crackers, noise and fire, in general, which can border on pyromania, was, and perhaps remains, ingrained in my soul. All the cautionary tales about three-fingered eight-year-olds would never change that.

To this nebulous, sprawling period of my life—those loosely-defined years of childhood that merge into one another—I owe my most puzzling and enduring memories, some magical, others enigmatic or disturbing: the green snake; the time I retreated into a world of dreams, losing all sense of time and place as I crawled underground.

I suffered for an entire year—sometime around my sixth or seventh—the bullying of a brutish clique of third-grade boys. Though admittedly not much older than I, they towered over me. In any case, it was always three-against-one.

In years to come, I'd attribute most of this misery to my own lack of discretion in speaking about the things I was not supposed to talk about at school: politics, and my father's once-secret meetings. Doña Gloria, a matronly laywoman—reputedly too proud to be a nun—on her right-hand ring-finger, a black stone to symbolize the heart she had privately pledged to her bridegroom, Christ— would ape my face back at me through the glass door that sealed off our playground. Refusing to intervene or even to let me through, she'd make mouths at me when I banged on the door and even as I squirmed on the ground, a dirty sole pressed against my cheek.

One day, I told my mother, who brushed it aside as something of no importance, then, ready to chide me, asked me what I had done. I came to believe, as the years went by, that growing up in a fascist world meant that one always expected to be in the wrong. All the same, she frowned and declared that she'd have a word with those boys. I actually feared for her safety, and I told her as much, to which she responded with seeming temerity, and something like disgust, that they were little—*just like me*. How little she understood...

As acting headmistress, Doña Gloria cast her shadow over me for what might have been years. It was she who always materialized when I was in trouble—the better to dish it out to me; she who stood over me in the dining hall, the day the children refused to eat their food; she who forced me, and me alone, to eat, while she watched with a sneer, as I gagged and vomited all over the floor. On hands and knees, I spooned it all back into the plate as ordered, and, for a tense moment, I feared that I'd really have to eat *that*. I didn't— though I suspect, to this day, that this had much to do with the timely arrival of my kindly second-grade teacher. For me and me alone, it became a daily ritual, which would end with a mess on the floor. The doctor called it acute gastroenteritis. My parents warned me, though, rightly suspecting the role of my own willfulness. Indeed, nothing was as unpalatable to me as being Doña Gloria's to command.

There were occasions, however, when I could—fondly, proudly, defiantly—see my mother as an ally against the powers that be; times also when my friends and I shared triumphs, gave free rein to our imaginations, like the week Eduardo told me about *piñones*—not pine nuts, in this case, as I learned, but bicycle gears—and we two, convinced that we had found the way to earn fame and fortune as inventors, spent entire afternoons drawing cars, bullet trains, planes, and rockets, all based on the principle of putting an exponentially growing number of gears in line. There was the day I shimmied up a lamppost to retrieve a multicolored scarf—thrown there by the equally diminutive but indomitable Victor—and I was rewarded with a kiss from a girl called Maite. I also emerged as the fastest runner in my grade. My talent reflected my temperament, more hare-than-tortoise-like. It also allowed me to get out of a few scrapes—useful, since I didn't seem destined to be one of the big boys.

But, best of all, there was the time my mother stood up for me—ironically, the day when I stood up for myself against school bullies, teachers and the world. It was also the last time that I ever had to cross paths with Doña Gloria.

It all started with a spate of name-calling and teasing in the playground. Some kids discovered that I would dissolve into incoherent rage when teased—unable to process or get my head around something that was never supposed to make sense. Didn't they *understand*? Couldn't they *see*? To be rebuffed yet again with waves of increasing laughter over a nonsensical nickname.

They'd shout it at the top of their lungs; repeat in a sing-song chant; screech it to apoplexy. They'd convulse with laughter, red-faced, beating the ground with their fists, while I sat down with my head in my hands.

After a few days of this, something snapped. It was the end of geography class when most of the children had already trooped out behind the teacher. One of the three Sergios brought the teasing into the classroom.

"*¡Piti-piti!*" He shouted inches from my ear.

As I yelled back, shaken and irate, I could feel the veins sticking out of my neck: "Shut up! Just shut your mouth, dickhead that you are—you-shitty-cuckold-son-of-a-whore!"

"*¡Piti-piti!*" A *second* Sergio hollered like a town-crier before he climbed onto a desk and swiftly tip-toed, one-table-to-the-next, the whole length of the classroom, all the while yelling the idiotic putdown about my small size.

No sooner had the second Sergio reached the end of the row and jumped down than Victor, no less, joined in the fun, ready to match the other boy's display, on the row of desks opposite. He swayed his hips left and right, and chanted in a girlie voice before running along the row of tables as I rushed toward him.

If you could call what followed a fight, it was the first one that I ever won—the only time I didn't end up tasting the dirt with one of his bony knees pinning my shoulder. Admittedly, it didn't involve much by way of grappling, *mano a mano*, but, then again, experience and instinct must have taught me that only artillery would do for Victor. Just as he reached the end of the row, so did the desk that I hurled across the classroom. He wasn't seriously hurt; as we say in Spain, "Bad weeds never die." Yelling like a maniac, I then chased Sergios I and II, swinging a chair around like a battleax—I had a whimpering boy cowering in the corner, a chair raised above my head when the teacher burst into the room: "*Por el amor de Dios, ¡Iván!*"

Odd as it may sound, I'm not sure whether it was my actions in that classroom, or my pigheaded refusal to *see the light*, that caused Doña Encarna to appeal to Doña Gloria herself, and, thence, for my mother to be summoned most urgently.

"But we tried to make him *comprehend*, to *see sense* and realize where he stands—to consider the model of our Lord and Savior— and when we told him that Jesus urged us to *turn the other cheek*, he had the *audacity* to answer back that *he was not Christ!*"

"Who *ever* heard such shamelessness," Doña Encarna pipes in.

"Yes," responds my mother. "That's absolutely right."

"Of course, of course, it is," the two *Doñas* reply, nodding sagely.

"I mean," clarifies my mother, her voice rising, "he told you the plain truth. He's *not* the Messiah. And let it be known that I will *not* bring him up to be some kind of *martyr!*" The last bit rolls off my mother's tongue like a dirty word. Their eyes, large and round like plates, are upon her, now; their mouths agape, their faces three shades paler.

"Well, I *never!*"

* * *

Later, I am heart-warmth incarnate. I'm floating ten feet above the ground, never mind walking on water. Mum brings me back to earth…

"And don't think that you've done no wrong!" she tells me, wagging her familiar stiff finger in my face. "Remember *the mouth*, Ivan—it's what I always tell you: *that mouth of yours will be your downfall.*

"*But*," I ask, a little confused. "*I* didn't start it—it was *their* mouths that called me things. Was I *supposed* to turn the other cheek after all?"

"*Iván*," she replies, exasperated. "I'm your mother, so listen up: don't be a simpleton!" She shakes her head, pauses, then, continues: "Of course, you had to stand up for yourself against those rude little shits. But you know better than to *answer back* when your teachers are chiding you!"

"But I didn't answer back. They asked. Wasn't I supposed to *reply?*"

"Ivan… *Iván*, are you trying to be difficult?"

I think it best to look contrite and say nothing.

"*But I am not Christ*", she parodies in a mincing tone. In my day, they would have thrashed you for that and had you kneeling with your arms spread and a thick Bible on each hand! You need to learn to say 'Yes, sir', 'No, Miss.' What *are* they teaching you in that school your father and I toil away to send you to?"

Keeping my mouth shut, I simply kept my head down like a good boy. But, without knowing it, at that moment in time, I might easily have been the living, breathing, eight-year-old embodiment of Spain's transition years.

I was gratified to hear the story repeated, and to see Mum more self-assured, possessed of more dignity and fire each time, her frowns reflected in the faces of the other women, her neighbors and fellow mothers. I was flattered to be the protagonist of my own life-story, and even to see my mother steal the lead.

"These religious-school laywomen are a hundred times worse than the clergy themselves!" explodes one of the other mothers. "*Sor Amalia* was very different", she adds, naming my preschool teacher of years past—the nun who had taught me to read and write. My ears are burning!

"She didn't hesitate to smack you sideways, to rap her knuckles across your *coco* if you were being a numbskull, or yank your ear off for not paying attention. But she was always fair, and she knew children and what they are like."

"Sor Amalia?" asks Mum, dumbfounded. "Why, she never hit Ivan…"

"Well, he must have gotten lucky. But my older brother… why, one time, who's Sor Amalia yanked one of his ears so hard that he required three stitches—and you can still see which one it was!"

Mum gasps: "Oh, my…." I succumb to a fit of nervous coughing.

"But, of course, those were other times," concludes our neighbor with one of those vague shrugs that mean everything and nothing at the same time.

* * *

Yes, it was definitely my mouth that got me into all sorts of trouble. Doña Gloria's vendetta aside, it is probably the 'Spitting-Jew Story' that best sums it up—along with my enquiries about local nationalism, and where *that* got me.

It may seem incredible, but, at that time, children aged eight-going-nine discussed—even argued about—politics. So, it was that I got into heated arguments, telling my peers that the Russians didn't all actually wear the same uniform, nor pray to the notorious Little Red Book when they sat down to a meal. They were actually friendly people, and, even if they were factory workers, they would go to the opera and the ballet—whatever that was. As if to prove the point, I showed off the brass Misha Bear sharpener and the giant, inch-thick pencil that Mum and Dad had brought back for us from their month-long trip to the USSR.

I also got into deep shit at school, for an offhanded—perhaps a wee bit scornful—question about a source of some controversy involving the local, Valencian flag.

"So, what is all this business about *'blau' or 'no blau'?*" I asked with disdain. Well, it was the debate about whether to add a blue stripe, to clearly distinguish the Valencian *senyera* from the flags of the other regions that once made up the sprawling medieval Kingdom of Aragon—and, particularly, from that of Catalonia to the north. My question was answered promptly.

"*Català!*" exclaims the first kid, slapping me hard across the back. Is it a joke—a friendly gesture, a little overdone? After all, backslapping was so popular that once I even caught myself backslapping a nine-month-old baby.

However, the second whack— delivered by someone else to the back of my head—relieves me, at once, of any doubts and of my chewing gum.

"*Català!*"

"But… but… I just wanted to *know* what all this blue-thing shit is about…. *What?!?*"

"The *Català* doesn't even know!" howls a third kid, with a mix of rage and exultation, as he delivers what we used to call a *soplamocos*—a generous whack that literally blows your nose for you. In my case, it knocked me off my feet. Fate had determined that I would take my beating lying down. A few kicks to rump and ribcage follow. I think I got out of that one quite easily, though, because, deep down, the kids were just kicking me out of frustration; they probably weren't quite sure what that whole *blau* controversy was about, either.

The "Spitting-Jew incident", however, is a pig of an entirely different color.

Perhaps, in these politically-correct, European Union times, a few things may have changed. But, back then, spitting was the standard way to express maximum disgust, and to soil and taint our enemies. And yet, somehow, it was open to universal condemnation. "Remember," boys were told, "girls spit and scratch when they fight." But the clincher was the Jewish thing. Spit at someone, as one would, and someone was sure to yell, ¡*Judío!*

Everyone used to know what that was all about. It was the old story about Jesus being spat upon by the other Jews while he bore his cross to Calvary. You can probably see where this is heading.

I knew the story, too, of course, but that was not going to stop me. I could almost hear my mother's warnings: remember the mouth, Ivan, *la boca*... But, I paid no attention.

"So, what's that shit about calling someone a Jew for spitting," I call out cockily from the back of the throng of heckling spectators at a playground fight.

"Huh?" The fight is immediately forgotten. It looks like thirty-three pairs of eyes are suddenly upon *me*. Was I being a smart-arse? Definitely. I was pretty full of myself at nine-and-a-half.

"You *know* ... how Jesus was spat on by the unbelieving Jews?... when he was being flogged like an *Ecce Homo*, and patiently bearing His cross...", somebody offers impatiently.

"But, wait," I shoot right back. "Wasn't Christ Jewish, too? I mean, I *suppose* that he was also *technically* the first Christian. But probably *not*, right? Because Christians should be humble, and you wouldn't expect Him to love Himself that much..."

There is a long moment of complete silence, allayed only by collective air-intake, while not a few rack their brains, and find words to soothe their offended souls, until muddled memories of *catecismo* lessons are distilled into the universal verdict of the lynch mob. "*BLASFEMIA!*" one explodes, a shaky finger levelled at me. The word is echoed and muttered by several others with different degrees of conviction.

"Not at all", I retort, head held high, still unable to see the shit I am in. "I mean..."

I got no further. I was knocked down and picked up again, slapped, punched, cuffed, kicked, walloped, whacked, whooped, stomped on, and generally given a good going-over. Nor was I forgiven seventy-seven times over. And, yes, there were kids aplenty—male and female, great and small—so enraged in their righteous souls, or perhaps simply caught up in the sheer joy of giving someone a good thrashing, that they did not hesitate to spit upon the crown of thorns that I had so imprudently placed upon my own head.

If only I'd listened to my mother...

The Green Viper and the Facts of Life.

I t was late spring. Beyond the school walls, the fields were yet to turn the color of hay—burnt to dust and ashes by the summer heat. Thoughts of the endless summer vacation were already upon us; the walls seemed higher, and I had seen boys run along their length. I marveled at their stubborn persistence to get there in the first place. They would tip-toe along, carefully, bending their heads down in anticipation, their bodies taut, as they readied themselves for the jump, and, finally, they would leap. I wondered if they stepped down onto the roof of a parked car and thence onto the asphalt. Rebels. How I envied them.

One day, a few minutes after morning recess, we hear a loud bang. At lunchtime, we race outside to find a large hole in the playground's wall. We are dumbfounded. *What* did it take to blow a hole the size of a large cinder-block clean out of the wall? We learn later that it had been the handiwork of some of the feared-but-revered eighth-graders. These kids were about to complete what was, at the time, the final year of E.G.B.—*Educación General Básica*—the leaving certificate. They had packed into a gap—surreptitiously picked out of the mortar in the wall—some red-foiled crackers, the largest *masclets* available in shops during Fallas. Perhaps they took their Pink Floyd a little too seriously.

Much as we were told to keep away from the hole, the management took a while to have it fixed, so, by the end, hardly any children in the place had resisted the temptation to stick their heads out, to peek at the fields beyond—a dusty country lane between two farms, bending to the left in the distance, the fresh light green of sprouting vegetables, the darker, earthier, more elemental greens and browns of reeds bordering the silty bubbling waters of the *acequia*. You could hear the hum of a tractor engine in the distance, the barking of a farmer's dog. Some of the younger kids could, in fact, squeeze through the hole, but this was no longer possible for me.

On the other hand, I could—*and did*—climb over the school's front gate. All I needed was a bit of a distraction, which older kids happily arranged while I embarked on an errand on their behalf, generally returning with cigarettes and the like. It was an exciting way to earn some attention. The older kids were otherwise an enigma.

One day, during one of the errands, I end up joining some older kids for a walk into the nearby *huerta*, where one of these kids' cousins—who is helping with the planting, I imagine—produces a large box. Without warning, I find myself pinned down, as two kids put all their weight on my calves while another leans on my torso to keep me from sitting up. My shorts and underwear are tossed carelessly over a disproportionate cabbage.

This is the position in which I find myself when the viper, arrow-like head of emerald, lidless eyes, piercing and impenetrable, slithers swiftly, as fluidly as a fish-in-water, between my tremulous legs, all gooseflesh. Each time, the snake, a green blur, seems about to reach its object, it is tugged back, as one would a rope, only to be released again, as I strain ineffectually against the arms that pinion me. I'm beyond screaming, too frightened to look but unable to take my eyes off the damned thing.

I never even told a soul about it—not for years, anyway. After all, I had been out-of-bounds during school hours, and I feared that

I'd get in trouble. When I did tell, years later, it must have seemed too incredible—the looks of disbelief said it all. At one point, even I had wandered if it could have really happened. I wasn't even sure if there were snakes in Spain. Hadn't they, perhaps, been led away, as in Ireland, by some saintly pied piper?

It was these boys, too—or, rather, others like them—who let me into the "Secret of Life", assuring me, that my mother and father had *sired me* by the passing of seed amid pig-squeals of pleasure. Oink-oink. ¡*Wheeeeeeek!* One of them even obliged me with a bestial squeal.

As hot tears scalded my eyes, I said, "No, no… it's not true," two of these kids—one lifting me physically off the ground by the lapels of my corduroy jacket, as the other pinched my groin—added that the *picha* would uncoil like the tail of a *cochino*, that swinish, rubbery corkscrew becoming a boar's tusk in no time. He squealed and grunted with gusto while his buddy bent down to breathe some words of reassurance:

"But, come on, now! Don't take it like that, *chiquet*. It's *all* of our parents, not just *yours*. Besides, in a couple of years, you too won't think of anything but *cochinadas* in here, either", he held my gaze with unblinking eyes, as he sagely patted his temple with two fingertips.

I follow their retreating figures with my eyes, suddenly unsteady on my feet, and I hear them chortle. They punch each other, poke each other in the ribs, the wind carrying their laughter to me: "Did you see the look on the little fucker's face?"

It is odd, considering that my cousins, raised a three-hour drive away, in a small village in the plains of La Mancha—dogs in their houses, half-wild housecats sneaking into the kitchen to snatch dinner, and flocks of sheep and goats that sow droppings up and down every street—have notions of sexuality far more realistic than my own, insulated city-boy ideas. And, yet, it may all be a matter of temperament or disposition. Part of what troubled me that day was a reawakened memory of something I'd seen a couple of years back in Mum's village.

"*¡Los perros agarraos!*" exclaims one of my aunts, as we turn the corner and see two yelping dogs roll onto their sides in the dust, bizarrely unable to pull apart.

"*¡No miréis!*" adds our grandmother, a little flustered.

Don't look? *Sure, Grandma...* While Luis and I are hastily led towards the dark-green portals—the key, quite heavy, and longer than an adult hand, already disappearing into a pocket of Grandma's dress—I twist to get a better look at what I'm not supposed to see, Grandma dragging me like a willful little goat.

An old woman in the perpetual mourning of those times, has now descended upon her own half of the canine couple. She utters something between a taunt and a reproach: "*Pero, ¡si tú ya estás viejo!*", as she flails her hapless hound with a birch broom. The no-longer-lucky dogs, struggle spasmodically to break apart free and flee the flailing fury of the unreasoning crone. Even then, as Luis and I cross the threshold into grandma's patio, a crowd of children—already half-frantic in the midday sun, all dirty hands and grubby faces—irrupt on the dirt street, pointing frantically, their laughter mingled with a spontaneous chant of "*¡Los perros agarraos! ¡Los perros agarraos!*" Luis and I can still hear them outside when the portal is firmly bolted inside.

* * *

However, always reliant on the word, spoken or written, until the day when I am told by the older boys of things that uncoil like pigs' tails, I had always believed, that even if babies *probably* were not brought by the stork (from Paris....), they were, somehow, sent by God to married people. At school, one of my classmates gravely assured me and a couple of girls who were there that the older kids' bestial utterances could be confidently ignored, though neither was conception simply the entirely innocent, divine blessing I believed it to be. Rather, it came from kissing, the key substance apparently found in saliva. I was dumbfounded. *Saliva...* who would have thought it? I was still puzzled. Hastily followed by her friend, Sandra, a precocious kisser, turned pale, and ran to the bathroom.

At home that evening, I cannot help but look at my parents differently. I ask a tentative question, shyly raising the things that those kids have said. I don't get very far, though, before I'm told to show more respect for my parents and elders, and told firmly, besides—a finger wagged in my face—that I should stand up for myself against insults and filthy kids. My parents are right, of course. I am sure that the fourteen-year olds would have known to keep away if I'd fought them.

A few nights later, strange noises originating down the long hallway keep me awake and whet my curiosity. I'm too afraid to get up and investigate. It sounds like furniture being moved, odd groans, drawers opened, a heated conversation conducted in whispers. The following morning, perhaps thinking myself too sly, I mention that I'd heard strange voices the night before— perhaps one of the neighbors had been sick?

I am tersely told to shut up, and told besides that nighttime is for sleeping. Both my parents seem flustered—Dad's eyes are literally bulging a little while Mum, her initial embarrassment quickly dissolving into irritation, looks as if she, in turn, might just reach for the dreaded slipper. Slaving away for my brother and I, and actually putting a roof over our heads and food on the table, they certainly don't need to deal with this shit, too.

I lower my head and I say "nothing" when pressed further with a couple of firm rhetorical questions. But I leave for school that morning feeling that my parents—though definitely not as bad as those of the horrible eighth-graders—were somewhat more beastly than I had ever imagined. All that remained for me now was to grow into a little pig, too.

Not long after, some older girls who sometimes treat me as their own kid brother—combing my hair with its straight fringe down to my eyebrows—and who give me sweets and ask me to read them their homework questions while they skip rope, pin me down for their favorite gag of tickling me purple. It usually makes me laugh to the verge of tears—not in a bad way. This one time, though, I burst into real tears, crying and yelling hysterically at my hapless, would-be older sisters, who cannot understand what has just happened. The teacher who materializes at the scene tells me to calm down, pats my back, and admonishes the girls to be less rough with the little ones. But, he also looks at me with an odd, puzzled frown before he walks away.

Marcelino

O f course, it's *possible* that he was simply named after someone in his family. But, given his character, I suspect that a pompous, matronly mother, or some church-devoted godmother, named him after the child-hero of the most successful film of the Franco years, a religious melodrama called *Marcelino, pan y vino* ("Marcelino, Bread and Wine", 1955).

My own given name was Russian, of course, and not yet common in Spain, as it would become in the '80s. To this day, I'm still thankful to my mother for putting her foot down and flatly refusing that I be called Vladimir.

Marcelino, in turn, could never live down the chants of *"Marcelino, pan y vino."* If Orwell's political fable had been an anticlerical satire, rather than a critique of political corruption and will-to-power, burly, sanctimonious Marcelino would have fit somewhere beside Napoleon and Squealer. *Marcelino, come-tocino* ("Bacon-Eater") and *Marcelino, cara-cochino* ("Hog-Face") seemed rather appropriate.

Marcelino and his older brother, Esteban, also stood out among other children, though for reasons different from my own. The eldest never spoke, save to "uphold the family honor", as he put it. At eleven, he would say this without a hint of irony.

Marcelino, in turn, was yet another odd child. He liked to talk as much as I did. It's not surprising, therefore, that we spent many-an-hour discussing—and arguing about—every subject imaginable, from the superiority of tigers over lions, to patriotism, to the Valencian flag, to our favorite books.

I don't remember exactly how it started. But, at some point, disagreements started to turn into arguments and name-calling, which would invariably culminate in references to our respective mothers. It simply had to happen, sooner or later. Well, after all these years, I must admit that, where he was concerned, the fault tended to fall on my side. I should also add that I was also guilty of being the shorter of the two by a head—which, in Marcelino's case, was disproportionately large, and topped with red hair above a pair of curiously fervent eyes.

After the first dismal fight, I no longer waited around to see my best punch glance off from rubbery torso or the wobbly butt he called a chin, and to be engulfed by his dumb girth. So, the endlessly repeated ritual would culminate in the timely demonstration of my skills as the best sprinter in my grade, a mad dash to safety in which I easily outstripped my hoggish *friend*.

But, alas! Esteban was another matter. He was a couple of years older, athletic, well-spoken and dutiful. I grudgingly admired him— he obviously took after his father, a disciplinarian of the military variety. Marcelino—sanctimonious by contrast, must have taken after some *beata* in the family, born to don an indented garter—like Doña Gloria presumably did—the better to mortify the flesh.

Like *déjà vu* for the hundredth time, there'd be an escalation of insults, Marcelino pausing—staring at me impatiently, as I racked my brain to come up with yet another insult; for one juicy enough, but *not* the one that really mattered—the one my honorable friend, deep down, *wanted* to hear.

I would catch myself thinking: "Here it comes … am I *really* doing this, one more time?"

"You dickhead! *Marcelino cara tocino.* You, son-of-the-Great-Whore!"

Shit—I've done it again!

After the first couple of times, Marcelino wouldn't even try to catch me. He'd simply march straight to summon his brother, who, I imagine, politely asked his friends to excuse him, as he abandoned a game of soccer or whatever—and joined the foxhunt.

I'd run to the next playground, sneak into one of the vacant classrooms—which were out of bounds during break-time. Once there, I'd gaze longingly out the window upon the playground below. I'd see them, too, like two hounds eagerly sniffing out my trail.

Sooner or later, I'd return to the playground, usually out of sheer boredom, and also due to the certainty that I had to face the music, sooner or later—the following day, the following week. Those two would never move on and simply let it pass.

Esteban, to be honest, never showed any personal animosity, and never sought to take The Law into his own hands—though this may have been the scariest thing about him. As an enforcer, he limited himself to ensuring that I faced Marcelino.

Sometimes, it was like a boxing match—both of us flailing wildly at Esteban's command. Other times, it was a bizarre duel, a ritualistic taking of turns, governed by the toss of a coin—dead dictator or anointed monarch giving Marcelino the first blow; tails letting me throw the first punch.

Why did I even bother talking to this guy, at all? I did think about it. But I never stopped because, sad as it may sound, there seemed to be no-one else whom I preferred to talk with.

* * *

The story of the guy with the handgun is also interesting. Eduardo and I were best friends for a month or two, as children will be. He was serious-looking and completely insane—just like me. Only, I had blond hair, soon to turn mousey brown, while his own was jet-black and hung in a long fringe, down to his eyes—this made us rather like the twin tearaways in the popular *Zipi y Zape* comic books.

Eduardo's father was a policeman, which is how he—a nine-year old—had been able to get his hands on a gun, *not* that it was his father's service pistol, or anything, since it looked small even in our childish hands. But, it seems remarkable, considering that guns were surely restricted in those years.

He showed me it during the morning break. He produced it from the pocket of his parka, as we stood in a cubicle in the bathroom. I fancied myself in an episode of *Starsky and Hutch*, or *Harrelson's Men*—shows we'd started to watch at friends' houses on the weekend. But, though I was *very* impressed, I wanted more. The bullets looked like tiny capsules of *gold*—brass, I guess; the grips in a dark wood; the rest, bluish steel. We loaded all the rounds, pushed the magazine home; Eduardo must have racked it or released a catch because I remember a satisfying click-clack, like on the cop dramas on television.

It was now ready to go, he explained. Powerful as the handgun was, much as it would kick back and bruise your hand, he explained, it could go off easily. It didn't require much strength, this being what was called *a hair-trigger*.

I urged him to fire at the ceiling, or at the wall, at least. After all, it had been *fallas* just a few weeks before—the smell and smoke of fireworks still in our lungs. *El 23 de febrero*—the gun in the air, the submachine-gun fire—also still fresh in our minds…

Just as well that he didn't listen to me. Instead, he put it away carefully, and later showed some other boys at the back of the classroom, pistol on the palm of an open hand, yellow bullets pinched between index and thumb for inspection.

It ended when one of the girls noticed. "You cannot bring *that* to class…"

She conferred with one of her friends. They nodded briefly together, and promptly marched, heads high, to the front of the class, the teacher's eyebrows rising sharply.

Eduardo got a serious dressing down. I was asked a string of questions—a soft-spoken teacher from another class extracting any information that I may have had. Eduardo's parents were called in. My own were also briefed.

At home again, I temporarily became a celebrity of sorts. I answered questions. I was fussed over.

One neighbor indignantly proposed that we have the man drummed out of the police force. Mum frowned, and pursed her lips. Dad swept it all aside, calling it a lot of childish nonsense. In fact, he spoke well of the police force, which he said served a legitimate function in any democratic society, and added that this man was a member of the *Policía Nacional*, not one of those *guardias civiles*— like Tejero *and company*—who lived in their barracks.

Needless to say, nothing really came of all this talk. But Eduardo and I were never as close as we had been after that day.

Religion and the Snake in the Garden.

T he *huerta* provided the backdrop to a substantial part of my childhood; we crossed it almost daily on the way to and from school. On those first days of school every year when summer refused to relinquish its hold on Valencia, we'd walk hurriedly along a well-trodden path, nothing but the rising heat blurring our perspectives, a hint of mirages and sand and madness, while the cicadas kept up the incessant whirring of their souls.

There was a short season when my own chatter during those walks home from school—the insistent jabbering, which never failed to entertain, engross or appall my mother, depending on my mood and her own—was suddenly stilled. Normally, I'd subject Mum to an endless string of questions, or share my latest obsession. There were, for instance, the stale, rancid restaurant leftovers that were being served at the school cafeteria: *restos* from the *restaurante*. I pointed out, a tad shrilly, that the word itself concealed the unsavory truth. Or, I'd talk about animals, and about my favorite sandwiches, or of the latest kid whom I couldn't stand. You name it, I chattered about it like a little monkey. Who knows, perhaps it was *good* to have a little peace and quiet, for once.

What I did, instead, is I started hanging back a little behind Mum and my younger brother. Softly muttering under my breath prayers of my own design, which I hoped to ward off the evil certain to befall those dear to me and wash me free of the guilt that surely engulfed me, and for which I'd never be able to forgive myself. These prayers all started the same way: "*Por favor, Dios y Jesus....*":

> Don't let anything bad happen to my Mum...
> Please, please, spare my little brother...
> Let Dad be happy and laugh a lot today...
> Make grandma and grandpa live for a long, long time...
> Oh—and, please, help me get *sobresaliente* in Geography.

One day, I got so distracted in my devotion that I nearly fell in a ditch, a mishap which I'd have undoubtedly addressed with a swift prayer to be safely delivered from the waters like Baby Moses from the Nile. Falling further behind, as I mumbled my prayers into the undergrowth, eyes half-closed in contemplation, pouting in penitent piety, I tested Mum's patience. She finally gripped my wrist and dragged me along.

"What are you moping about, now?" She asks, a frown edged across her brow. "Did you get into a fight at school?" (The latter punctuated was by a hand-squeeze).

"No. It's nothing...."

"Are you *sure*?" Her gaze bores into my eyes, which I lower in confusion and distress; for, I am firmly convinced that—rather like New Year's wishes—to reveal the subject of my prayers would cause them not to come true.

It must have been sometime in my ninth year that I underwent this sudden conversion to godliness, which is quite a feat, considering that I'd attended religious schools since the age of three—taught by nuns as a preschooler, no less. There, the children had been instructed about the cardinal rules: to be kind to others; to pay attention to the nuns; to consider all little creatures as worthy of life, even the little ants. The nuns weren't terribly amused though when one of my little friends added some other creatures, such as cockroaches, rats and centipedes to the list of wonderful creatures that should be spared because God had made them. We'd also been taught to eat all our food: mashed potatoes, yellow egg-noodle soup, and soupy rice of a similar hue, on a three-day cycle. This was our *job*, just as our parents worked to feed us, clothe us and send us to school.

Scripture and the niceties of theology were evidently not at the top of their list of priorities, as shown when I—with that self-importance so endearing at four or five, so repulsive at seven or eight—informed *Sor* Amalia that people didn't have two lungs, but only one, much larger than the mysterious white organ on the left side, which, in fact, was *the soul itself!* She nodded, recognizing me for a precocious sage. Then, she led me—a quiet little smile on her face—so that I might tell her sisters, who were similarly impressed. I have wondered since if perhaps I reminded them of their bishop.

Mum and Dad set me straight, of course, insisting that there *really* were two lungs in the human chest. But, I wasn't too convinced because their explanation about what the soul *was*—and, most importantly, about *where* it might be—seemed vague and dubious to say the least.

Later, at a primary school affiliated to the preschool, our lay teachers—some of whom seemed paradoxically more zealous than the nuns, particularly during the weekly scripture class—soon aroused in me an instinctive, but deep-dyed, sense of distrust and distaste for the whole thing.

The war, however, was far from over. At some point during the third grade, Don Fernando, a teacher so passionate about his profession that he'd forget what he was supposed to be talking about, as his digressions *became* the lesson, opened the door for the nearly forty rapt children to a whole world full of wonders. It was then that I started to pay attention even to those things I'd always considered stuff for little girls. Foremost among those—even above music, at which I was quite hopeless—had been *catecismo*.

It was not the scripture lessons themselves, either, but the little booklets that I was given one day—promotional things, introducing readers to a serialized collection. Decked with tinfoil borders, in silver and gold, these *fascículos*, or "instalments", were illustrated little Bible stories—and I, who had been hooked on reading since preschool! Clever bastards; I didn't stand a chance…

It wasn't fire and brimstone, much as I'd heard tales of flames that are never quenched, and of the souls and bodies of sinners, which will burn for eternity and yet never be consumed.

Nor was it the concept of forgiveness and salvation, nor the mix of guilt and gratitude inspired by the Messiah's personal sacrifice, though the concept of the Golden Rule—to do unto others, and so forth—seemed to be the most sensible aspect of the Christian faith.

It is quite simple, really. It was SEX.

One of the booklets retold the tale of "Jesus and the Penitent Woman in the house of the Pharisee." We'd been read something about an adulteress, which illustrated our need to be forgiving since none of us is above making mistakes. But, this was something else. In all my young years, I had simply *never* read anything quite so … *appealing.*

It was this image of a gorgeous girl on her hands and knees, weeping scalding-hot remorseful tears upon My divine feet—a little sore from walking all over rocky Palestine; it *was* her cascading tresses straight out of *Charlie's Angels*, from which the seraphic, adoring face of one of the Yolandas gazed out, and her hair, so silky and soft—though, now, a little grubby—having just scrubbed and anointed said sore feet, while I gazed benignly down upon her, and told her that all this wasn't really necessary.

It was nice to be the Messiah.

Deep down, I didn't want to be a Christian, so much as I wanted to be *the* Christ—all except for the part about Calvary, I suppose. At that point, I much preferred Peter, hacking off a Roman centurion's ear. Peter was my favorite apostle, even for his human failings—his denial of Christ thrice before cockcrow the stuff of high drama. He could not be outdone, however much the *catequista* enthused about Saul/Paul, the former Christian-hunter, because, to me, his conversion smelled too much of self-serving hypocrisy, much like the phony reverence and spirituality put on during this class by eight-year olds—myself included—to earn the teacher's favor.

It may sound, of course, as if I have just confessed my conversion to the Church of the Blaspheming Mouth. But, it was not like that, at all. Once my defenses were down, once I'd accepted the essential greatness of this man, Jesus—reflected in such adoration from genuine guys, like Peter, and adorable babes, like the long-haired adulteress—the rest was inevitable.

Soon, I was reading scripture in my spare time. In fact, I started keeping a growing stash of those little booklets in an old biscuit tin, where I also kept old buttons, stamps, pictures—and a stocking-full of infantile poems, neatly folded into infinitely small packages. There, too, were the coins I *retrieved* from around the house with ne'er-a-scruple, in my days of innocence, for sweets and such things. At night, now, in my sleepless bed, these ill-gotten gains became the object of feverish prayers for forgiveness, though, ironically enough, I never returned the money. Rather, I would spend it at the same kiosk where schoolkids bought sweets, firecrackers and loose cigarettes. There, I would piously trade my thirty pieces for more of those same illustrated scripture books.

Underground in the Belly of the School

I t must have been one of those long, exhausting days in early autumn, summer's last rage, the sun beating down upon the children in the playground, that I discovered the way into the belly of the beast. A small, grilled trapdoor of sorts, never properly secured, gained me access, while I played a savage version of hide-and-go-seek with those two fierce brothers, who were bent on avenging my daily affronts. It seems bizarre, now. I must have gone underground right under people's noses. But I remember nothing about that, as if, in the middle of a busy thoroughfare, an office worker should lift a manhole cover and descend into the dark, and nobody noticed, or cared enough to think of it, or to utter a word.

Through the grate, I watch the two hunters run back and forth. They search the toilets, stare into the faces of various children, puzzled about how I could have regained the playground from which they'd just come. That day, I went no further. I came out on hands and knees, straightened up and dusted myself down, though unable to get the peculiar smell of old dust, damp, and, as I fancied, death, out of my nostrils.

I returned with two others—friends this time. The deeper we went into the underside of the school building, the darker it all was, but, as our eyes grew accustomed to the dark, it wasn't too difficult to find our way. Besides, in the dark, our other senses were sharpened. We listened intently to each other, to the noises proceeding from outside; the noises of pipes, of wiring, the oddly whistling air currents that somehow occurred in such a seemingly hermetic space. The cool air raised goose-bumps, fear, no doubt, playing a role. It was, ultimately, how we listened not so much to each other as to ourselves, as we disconnected from the game—in which we'd chased each other, slithering like reptiles on our bellies, or like assassins on each other's heels. We had also thrown and retrieved a river pebble much like a smallish egg, smooth and cold to the touch.

The most uncomfortable thing, perhaps, was the distinct sense of being trapped, for the slab ceiling above us seemed to grow progressively closer. Buried alive, entombed in silence the farther we moved within, we dragged ourselves on our bellies, in that solitary, desolate no-mans-land, detached from the playground that we had left behind.

I am not entirely certain whether the adventure was repeated, though it is the nature of children, or, at least of the kind of child that I know I was, to have done so, as with a ritual. Attuned to my own feelings, I suddenly realized that my companions had left me—perhaps afraid of being locked in, or of losing their way, or of getting caught as they came out, or of staining their clothes or their attendance records by emerging too late for the next lesson. They may have voiced some of these concerns, to me. Then again, perhaps it was no-one but myself and my own thoughts. I grew tired, remembered tales of the miners and their caged birds, the gas that puts you to sleep, the snow that is at first unpleasant, but, which, robbing you of enough of your vital heat—breathing the chill of death into your lifeblood—lulls you into a tender sleep from which none do rise, as Pluto takes you for himself. I dreamt awake of those sleepers in the tale, who rose again after one hundred years, and although, as I lay there, a long shiver traveled up my spine and raised the hairs on the back of my neck, I found that I lacked the power to rouse myself. So, I stayed, immobile, for an indefinite length of time while the noises from the outside world grew ever more faint, even as my breath grew labored, then, simply calm, almost still altogether, and my living dream gave way to that heavy sleep of childhood, which is filled with vivid dreams and with the lethargy enjoyed only by those who live, as yet, untouched by time. The waking dream and the dreaming of the sleep of childhood merged into one another, just as my memories of this period defy the boundaries of the present, yet could be no other way.

Child of the catacombs, the damp crept into my bones; curling up, I brought my knees up to my chin, dreamt of the quiet places of the past: the silence of ill-fated Pompeii; of caves; of mine-shafts; of graves. I dreamt of a sleek black dog, my grandfather's faithful companion, which I, too, had loved; one that now gave life to an olive tree, whose roots, limb-like, embraced its bones, as it had perhaps—in a life both greater and lesser—once received homage and rendered equal duty to the fallen warriors and the worn-out slaves of former ages.

When I emerging from the depths, I realized that the sun was no longer where it had been, that there was a chill in the air that seemed at odds with the torrid heat of the open playground prior to our descent into the building's dank, funereal underbelly. The morning break had passed—so, too, had the long afternoon lunch break. No-one had noticed me missing; I had simply vanished unnoticed, without importance.

Indeed, as I emerged, I realized that my clothes, scuffed and grey with fine dust, hung upon me, as if a long time had passed down there, long enough for my body to have shrunk within its woven skin, and my mouth, dry and tight around my chattering teeth, tasted of dust and ashes.

I walked out, unnoticed, and the trapdoor behind me sprung shut to become barely visible again. Merging with the worn bricks, it seemed too small to admit human entry. I made my way across the playground, feeling woozy and somnolent, as I made my way back to my classroom upstairs with a faint, wheezing cough by which to remember it all.

"Where have you been?" asked my teacher, Don Fernando, who seemed a little shocked, but seemed oddly concerned. I later understood that I must have looked quite a sight. I nodded by way of apology, coughed, replied that I'd gotten lost, that I'd been trapped below ground, like the little boy in the well the previous year— the one who'd died, I thought, not the one who hid while others, a whole nation, sought him, and mourned his parents' loss. Then, misunderstood, by myself as by all besides, I wept quietly, and was led to the school infirmary.

At home, I was quiet, thoughtful. My parents looked at me with puzzled eyes when I seemed to be lost in thought at the dinner table. They were concerned that I needed more rest, and urged me to go to bed early, and not to stay up reading. But, left to my own devices, I soon disobeyed. Through conscious of a certain strangeness in myself, I instinctively grasped that my solitary engagement with books—which had gone some way to *dry my brain*, as Cervantes happily put it—was, paradoxically, also my means of once again reconnecting with the words—and hence the world—of others.

Velez-Rubio, Almería

We travelled all day. A woman, whose age I'm not sure about, but must have been old, wanted to see her birthplace. Decades before, in her childhood, she and her parents, now long-since dead, had fled Franco's advance in the South. It was one hell of a long drive from Valencia, and it took us pretty much all day—my first time travelling in that region.

These days, the south-west of the peninsula is known for large-scale greenhouse-agriculture—the largest such set-up in all of Europe, it produces massive amounts of market vegetables, and even such things as kiwi fruit, once unknown on Spanish tables. Back then, however, it was one of the poorest regions in Spain, best known for its arid terrain—a desert so much like that U.S.-Mexican border region of the popular imagination that it was used as a cheap alternative in such Italian-produced *spaghetti westerns* as the ones that launched the career of Clint Eastwood: *For a Fistful of Dollars*, *The Good, the bad and the Ugly*, and many others in the '60s and '70s.

We drove all day, spent a couple of hours travelling through a sea of Andalusian olive trees that extended to the horizon—trees gnarled with time, known as they are for their longevity. The things that must have happened under their eternal shade …

We stopped for lunch at a roadside diner. Someone suggested a nice bit of soup—nothing like some home cooking. The lady at the pit-stop must have run out of noodles—or, else, she really was the most miserly person we'd ever met. Everyone, at some point in time, must have added a little more water to make the soup go further—but this was ridiculous. The sight of the watery chicken stock with a measly offering of scattered noodles floating, here and there, conjured up the proverbial "four noodles dancing" in the broth. It was enough to make your stomach heave. In my family ever since that day, anytime we've had insufficient ingredients to make a particular meal, it has brought to mind that miserly soup.

When we finally arrived after travelling all day, the lady looked around the town square and the major streets that stretched in four directions, and she clearly was as much a stranger to the place as the rest of us. She didn't know what else to look at or look for, and had no-one left to call on. She probably hadn't started out with any great illusions—had merely wanted to see the place where she'd been born, and where her people, whom she'd lost such a long time ago, harked from. But, once there, it was even less meaningful than she had envisaged. There appeared to be no remaining bond between her and that particular corner of Spain. So much for our journey to Velez-Rubio, Almería. After a couple of minutes, as this sank in, she turned to us: "Shall we go back?"

The Witch Train

In the rural region of La Mancha, where both my parents were born, the fairs would run during the hottest part of the year, especially the days leading to the fifteenth of August—a feast day in many localities, including Mum's hometown.

During those long summer afternoons—when there's daylight until after 8.00—we'd all drive out of Mum's small village to attend one of the country fairs in one of the larger towns not too far away. The early afternoon was dominated by raffles, shooting booths, rides, food-stands, teddy bears and novelty items, such as those really cool, little, plastic toy trumpets that we promptly blew into the nearest eardrum. Music would blare out of every stall in the place. The one year that I especially remember was dominated by one tune: "*Los pajaritos*", also known as "The Chicken Dance", but with Spanish lyrics, and performed by a local, accordion-wielding performer who became a national celebrity that year. One of my aunts—the heftiest woman in the family since time immemorial—even got down to dance with the little kids. In response to the line about moving one's *colita*, she squatted down to swivel her ponderous behind, side-to-side—little tail, my butt!

In the evening we'd improvise fairground dinners out of char-grilled sardines, *chorizos*, and the ubiquitous *blanco y negro*—a bread-roll stuffed with an ordinary, white sausage and a *morcilla*—the smoked, blood-and-onion one.

I also remember riding the bumper car. We call them *coches de choque*, literally "crash cars." To properly translate the *dodgem* name would have also been to adopt an alien philosophy about those things. But, if you always dodge, where would be the fun in that?

Years before, my younger brother—only three or four at the time—had gotten the worst of it when a teenage couple rammed the back of the car that he and Mum were in. He'd come out of his first traffic accident with a fat lip, which I somehow couldn't help but feel guilty about when I looked at him. But, he *had* gotten some free ice-cream from the guy in charge, who'd been very apologetic.

But riding the bumper cars was nothing next to the Witch Train. *El trén de la brujas* was one of the most memorable rides a kid could ever climb onto in a country fair, and I must have done so a few times as a child.

The Witch Train was your classic kiddy train, which takes you through tunnels festooned with bats, and which features a soundtrack of howls, maniacal laughter and blood-curdling shrieks. The actual witches were the icing on the cake, though. The good ones would give you balloons on sticks—and even the helium-filled ones, which made us talk funny. But, the result was the same: as we emerged from the next dark tunnel, there'd be a bunch of *bad* witches. You could tell because even their lipstick was black. Anyway, you knew which kind they were soon enough because they'd go for your balloons with their long knitting needles—no fear of poked eyeballs and lawsuits, in those days! The younger kids would burst into tears... I retain a vivid memory of a younger child, breaking out into the bright smile of unutterable joy, a feeling dashed a minute later, the kid's face crumpling abruptly into inarticulate woe. That's just how it was. Sometimes, you were lucky and you still had a balloon, at the end. But, big or small, you couldn't count on it.

We wouldn't just be there in the daytime, of course. We'd sometimes stay well into the night, even past midnight and into the wee hours, the chill which my grandfather inexplicably called "*la marea*" (the *tide*), noticeable only sometime after that. If we stayed that late, well, then, everybody, young and old, had an excuse to celebrate with hot chocolate and *churros* powdered with sugar and cinnamon.

I remember welcoming the year 1979 just like that. Under what was, properly speaking, a circus tarp, we embraced, yelled "happy New Year" to all and sundry, kissed and were kissed by everyone. New Year's always means that it's four weeks to my birthday. That year, it would be my seventh.

Thick, hot chocolate still sliding into my belly, biting into the oily remnants of my last *churro*, I walked around the merry-go-round and past a large Ferris-wheel that went up at an odd angle into the sky. Nothing too fancy, mind you. I still hadn't even come across a roller-coaster—though we knew of them from TV shows, and called them *montañas rusas* ("Russian mountains"), even though we knew that it was an invention from America. My mum also told me that some stupid rich people in Spain put peroxide—the bubbling cure-all for all my cuts and scrapes—in their children's hair to make them as blond as the kids in the American TV shows, and their hair was burnt dry like the *esparto* grass that Grandad wove into chair-bottoms.

I couldn't find the toilet. Was there even one? In Mum's hometown, where her whole side of the family still lived, we were still weeing into a pisspot every night—*everybody* was, never mind how rich or poor. Town water and a modern sewage system only came in a year or two later, along with paved streets. So, I'm not sure that there really *was* a bathroom there to begin with. No matter. I ran behind the big tent, where they'd set up the hall of mirrors, and, then, I sneaked behind a huge parked truck. I could hear the music. So, I knew that Mum and Dad and everyone were just on the other side.

And so, I take it out, quick as I can, and I start to pee—like a fire-hose—and, well, if I'm going to pee, I might as well pee against this giant semi-trailer tire, right here—which practically comes up to my chest—or against the nearest fencepost, column, or tree I can find. In fact, even dogs know about these things, although the reason why they stick out their leg when they do is a totally different matter. As I'd been told by someone with a good poker face, dogs do that because of the fate of the first dog which ever peed on a wall and didn't stick its leg... so, the wall fell on it!

I'm slashing away, playing swordfights with my own shadow. I daydream about our nightly ritual—usually followed by Grandma, or Mum, chiding us, and pouring a bucket of well-drawn water. Luis and I, along with Antonito and Jacintín—four cousins in line— piss down the sloping porch at Grandma's house, steaming rivulets rolling towards the towering coach doors. Which one will get there first? Antonito, I'm convinced, holds it in all afternoon, just with this competition in mind. This one time, though, his *meá* meandered to join mine, which, increasing in size with this new supply of yellow juice, forged ahead to win the day. He did not agree, though, but insisted that *my* rivulet was clearly absorbed by his own, a mere tributary to his triumphant torrent.

"Eeeeeewww!" he's weeing in the street, Marga!" shrieks some countryside *infanta* of around my own tender years. Another girl, maybe an older sister or cousin, shakes her head in shared disapproval.

"What a *disgusting* boy!" Squeals the princess, still not taking her eyes off the mini-wiener, which I am helpless to do anything about, turning off the flow not being so easy when you've been holding it in since four-thirty. And—*voilà!*—she's joined by two or three of her kin, all crinkling their noses and uttering a collective "*eeeek!*"

So, getting to the bottom-of-the-bladder, now, I swirl around, crying out "Ha, ha!", and spray a swift jet across their lacey-skirted ankles—with that fine stuff dragged across the dust and dirt of the *feria*, they shouldn't care too much, right? But, just in case, I turn quick as a flash and run as fast as my little legs will take me, lest the shrieking bluebloods have any brothers—or retainers—to take it up with me, my ears still ringing from the yells and shouted threats behind me, which must be reaching the heavens.

I scamper away and get back to the tent where my parents—along with my uncles, aunts, *primos* and *primas*, young and old, one and all—had moved to enjoy yet more food and drink till sunup. And, so, I run into the final year of the '70s.

Strangers

My mother's village is located in the plains of La Mancha, an arid area known for harsh winters and scorching summers. It is Don Quixote's own land: a few miles from Dulcinea's village of El Toboso, and a half-day's mule-ride from the Campo de Criptana, on the arid plains where Cervantes' knight-errant took windmills for giants.

Not surprisingly, the custom of the siesta was traditionally followed—a largely agricultural community knowing that taking a break from fieldwork after lunch, in the middle of a backbreaking, fourteen-hour summer day—was the only sane thing to do.

Seen from the distance as one travels across the plains, a village looks like shallow mound in the horizon with a solitary apex in the middle: the bell-tower of the local church. In the case of my mother's village, you would see *two*; for, small as it is, the village was historically divided into two halves. One half—where my mother's family was from—was once the domain of a powerful marquis while the other had belonged to one of the religious orders of knighthood formed during the Christian *Reconquista*, which lasted some eight-hundred years. To this day, each side of the village has its own parish church. When a country road was built, dividing the village in two, it gave a tangible modern confirmation to that traditional division.

In times past, such was people's attachment to their *patria chica*—a sense of belonging to one's *little homeland* comparable to the excesses of nationalist fervor—that it was very rare, up until the time of my mother's own parents and older siblings, for a young person to marry someone from the other side of the village, much less someone from another town— a *forastero* or outsider; as they'd say in Westerns, a *stranger*.

Young men, in particular, would watch *their* girls jealously, to keep interlopers from poaching the limited supply of marriageable women. My grandmother told me of how even older, local men— typically widowers who remarried, thus, taking one of those available women—would be mocked, even downright harassed by the rowdy local bachelors, who might bang pots and pans outside the windows during the wedding night. It is probably no coincidence, therefore, that both my grandparents came from the same side of the road.

In the case of my brother and I, visiting in the summertime, our cousins would clarify our identity to local children who would, then, welcome us with warmth and generosity.

In our grandparents' house, bunches of grapes dried to perfection, hung from hooks in the beams of the kitchen ceiling, near a sturdy, rough-hewn, vinyl-covered table. Luis, aged three or so, looked quizzically up one day and asked with the words of an older man, "So, when do we get the grapes around here?" Our eldest uncle, laughing, got to his feet, with a compliment to the child's precocious character: "Right away, *¡chavalote!*", and hoisted Luis on his shoulders to unhook a nice bunch, which we all shared on the spot with some country bread and a slices of manchego cheese.

In those days, the village was a place of whitewashed houses, daubed with quicklime each year to keep the elements out of walls made of beaten earth. Houses left unattended for some time, as the younger generations sought work in the larger towns and cities, would quickly start to crumble, walls collapsing in a matter of years. Village life had probably been much the same for hundreds of years, the village itself seemingly eternal—winding, narrow dirt-streets lined with whitewashed houses around churches that were built out of unhewn, local stone, in the fifteenth and sixteenth centuries—but which was only ever a fragile presence, requiring constant care and upkeep.

When I was last there, aged in my mid-twenties after an absence of many years, my grandfather, one of the last survivors of his generation, led me on a melancholy walk around the outskirts of the village, the collapse of old family homes a common sight.

But, it was during my childhood—in 1980, to be precise—that the ancestral custom of drawing water from the nearest public well—using a winch and a bucket, just like it had always been done—was finally abandoned. My grandfather ploughed his fields using mules until his retirement when he acquired a car and a license to drive it.

The forces of progress and prosperity, given momentum by the transition to democracy, saw the introduction of running water and modern plumbing to the village, as well as the end of those unsealed streets, where householders had formerly swept the front of their houses and sprinkled water onto the dry summer dust before sitting on small wicker chairs to talk to their neighbors across the narrow street long into the night.

But, at festival time, locals would eye visitors coming to town with suspicion. Do you know those people over there? Are they related to so-and-so? No—they must be *forasteros*...

Perhaps they'd come from a village eight or ten miles down the road, a village no different to their own in any serious way.

Of course, not so long ago, many people saw little reason to travel along that road, at all, and would visit the larger provincial towns only when they had a special need for it. I remember one of our own aunts, who had to travel some fourteen kilometers to buy a new dress to wear to a wedding. She got into the car nervously, crossing herself, and when she returned, three or four hours later, puffed out with relief: "Ouf! It's good to be back home, in the village." She embodied an old attitude that had always been part of the local culture.

Years later, in her old age, carrying her own cellphone, she'd go on coach trips all over the country with other retirees, and years before that had attended literacy and numeracy classes in her late-forties, which helped her to better manage the family finances, lands and other matters, and thus, avoid some of the pitfalls into which the uneducated easily fall.

In that context, my brother and I occupied a special place, belonging to the town by virtue of our parentage and our kinship with dozens of people in that community—in other words, not *forasteros*, in the true sense of the word. Yet, raised in a modern city, our own lives were totally alien to the lives of our cousins.

Village life always had its advantages and disadvantages—a place where one belonged, but which was potentially stifling, people trapped in relationships with an extended family of sorts, or, perhaps unable to escape the past.

Our own parents belonged to a great generation of people who left their rural communities for the big cities, or for foreign lands, in search of a better life—they were part of the rural exodus of the fifties and sixties, which, in a sense, has never really ended. When my father, fifteen at the time, left his provincial hometown for Valencia, he was very much a young man of his generation. One year later, when he exchanged Spain for France along with his parents and siblings for a decade, he established a life-pattern of migration that would one day take us all to Australia.

Perhaps my father's left-handedness might have gotten repressed anywhere, but I suspect that growing up *en provincias* made it worse. He holds his pen in his right hand because the teacher thrashed him out of using his left; he holds his spoon in his right hand because my grandmother enforced conformity using the same technique. As a carpenter, he holds his hammer in his left hand, as Nature intended.

But, perhaps, my mother's village—far smaller than my father's birthplace—presented increased possibilities both for the good and the bad sides of small-town life: the shelter and the impossibility of change. There, a childish prank, someone you answered back too pertly, a memorable playground fight, the scar that you gave so-and-so, could follow you forever, your identity inscribed in the local mind.

Parents would often chide their children to enforce the manifold norms of conformity to keep gossip at bay and idle tongues from wagging. What am I going to do with this child? Don't you have any *malicia*, Ivan? "Malice"? Yes, but not quite. In this case, *malicia* means cunning, shrewdness—the opposite of being *inocente*, or, rather, *un inocente*—an innocent—which, in this context, is tantamount to calling someone a simpleton.

There are sayings and adages for every sentiment; one proverb will recommend a particular attitude or course of action while another contradicts the first one. But a pattern seems to emerge, one that encourages pragmatism and caution with a tendency towards a cynical, sardonic take on life and human nature. The result is an ethos of survival based on rather mean-spirited conformity, accompanied by plain distrust.

Of course, there is one proverb that says: *Piensa el ladrón que todos son de su condición*—the thief thinks that everyone is like him; in other words, evildoers always think the worst of others. But, an even better-known one states, *Piensa mal y acertarás*: "think ill, and you will guess correctly."

For me, the result of this way of thinking was illustrated the day when one of my cousins helped a neighbor who'd locked herself out of the house, leaving a baby inside. Now, I should add that this was not the homeowner—middle-aged and decked out in the dreary mourning clothes of countrywomen of a certain age. This was her cute teenage daughter, babysitting a younger brother. So, my cousin—a teenager at that time, but already working as a farm laborer—threw off his jacket and climbed, bare-hands gripping a drain-pipe, and along a railing to the open, upper-floor window. The girl was reunited with her baby brother in no time.

While his friends—and the girl in question—saw him as a very cool, gallant type, who'd come to the rescue, my aunt wasn't too happy when she found out. Had he taken leave of his senses? This child of hers had none of the *malicia* needed to survive in a small town.

You don't go out of your way to attract attention. Start drawing attention to yourself, and, next thing you know, *you* will have to explain yourself.

The older generations were always eager to avoid drawing attention to themselves, lest someone reprehend them. They would urge their kids to be careful and watch themselves. "*¡No nos vayan a llamar la atención!*" The fear was, literally, of being singled out and reminded to conform. As a child, I'd muse about the meaning, imagining an authority figure yelling out: "Hey! You there!"

My grandfather once saved a man's life. The man, in desperate straits during the famine that followed the Civil War, and, seeing no other way out, had attempted to put an end to his problems using a thick rope and an olive tree. Like many suicidal people, he got had a change of heart the instant his feet no longer supported him.

Fortunately for him, my grandfather was on his way to the next village with a cartload of firewood, accompanied by other carters, and they saw him in the nick of time, the man's legs still kicking spasmodically. Grandad supported the man's weight on his own shoulders and quickly cut through the rope; countrymen in those days typically tucked a folding-knife in their waistbands.

Ashamed to see her husband delivered to her with a red welt around his neck, however, the man's wife, no doubt fearful of the gossip that would ensue—and with a priest in the family, too— almost immediately began to raise malicious doubts about the fact that carters also used rope to tie down their loads, and from that it was but a short step to insinuate that my grandfather may have attempted to kill her husband by hanging! Luckily, before things became more complicated, her husband regained his voice and his conscience, and admitted the truth.

As Grandad told us this story, and joked about the lesson he'd learnt that day, long ago, Grandma and her friends, sitting around, chuckled along, but also nodded shrewdly at each other. *What had he been thinking, anyway—meddling like that in other people's affairs?* Grandad had been *lucky*....

So, in the same time-honored way, my aunt reproached her son. Imagine if someone else came along and broke into a couple of houses. Never mind that any number of young people around the place might have been strong and athletic enough to do the same. But, it might simply have been the unconventional nature of his actions—a lack of *decorum*. Such a stifling demand to fit in, to conform. So much for the neighborliness and hospitality of the countryside! If things seemed oddly repressive even to my childish mind, on vacation in the countryside, I could imagine what it must have been like for my parents to live in such a culture in times far worse—the 1940s and '50s, when they had grown up in such small communities, as the children of those who had lost the war against the landowning elite and their lackeys.

La URRSSS

The summer our parents spent a month in the Soviet Union—*la URRSSS*, since plurals get double initials in Spanish—Luis and I stayed in Mum's village with our grandparents and the whole side of her family. It was 1979, just a few months before the Moscow Olympics, which is why the souvenirs that Mum and Dad brought back included a lot of Olympic-themed stuff.

Imagine me aged seven. The neighbors wanted to know where Mum and Dad had gone for their holiday. I promptly spilled my guts, revealing what I knew—pretty much everything. I was always a good listener—I just didn't listen to Mum's imprecations to be more discreet. So, the inquisitive neighbors—wide-eyed and open-mouthed—promptly knew that my parents were originally going to visit Romania, but that a last-minute change of plans meant that they and the party friends with whom they were traveling, had gone to Russia, instead.

Grandma pulled me aside the minute we were out the door. She confirmed exactly what I'd told them. *What? How? Who?*

The instructions were clear: if *anybody* else asked—and they *would*, of course—I was to tell them that I didn't know. Just shrug and say that they'd gone on a holiday to the seaside...

- *¿De acuerdo?*
- *Claro que sí, abuelita.*

Yet, Grandma must have known that no-one else needed be told. News travels fast in a little place, where there's nothing much to do but gossip about other people's business. It was hardly the 1930s when Spanish intellectuals had made the unheard-of-trip into Bolshevik territory. But word got around, anyway.

The next day, Luis and I were playing in the front patio, which originally housed the old cart, replaced for a few years by a small car. We were playing dominoes when we heard a lot of noise outside. Female voices rose in a penetrating cry: "¡*Dah-miah-naaaahhhh!* They're painting your portals red!"

Luis and I started up and ran towards the door, but Grandma, rushing from the rear, overtook us, flushed in the face, panting. We let her through.

As soon as she threw the door wide, Luis and I practically hanging onto her apron-strings, we heard the laughter of three female neighbours—the harsh squawking of crows. I yelled "*Urracas!*" at them—magpies. Dressed head-to-foot in regulation mourning, they looked the part. Showing off their missing teeth and their ignorance, they turned away, tears rolling down their cheeks, while Grandma, her arms around us, hustled us back over the threshold. "Pay no attention. They are very bad…"

Luis, squirming and twisting around to glare at them over Grandma's shoulder, the telltale vein in his neck, shook with rage "*¡Jilipollas!*" He yelled after them. "*japutas!*"

Grandma had carried us in. But, even as she turned to get the wooden wedge that kept the door from rattling at night, Luis ran back outside to hurl a half-brick: "*Pero, ¡habráse visto! El muchacho…*" The crones scurried away from the six-year old: "Ever seen such a thing? That boy…"

I remember the beautiful slides that Mum and Dad brought back from that trip, and many others they took during those years— their generation truly in love with positive film. Some were taken much closer to home. One of them showed my cousin, eight, arm frozen in motion forever, as his hand cut an arc to strike the rabbit he held by its hind legs, the blow to the nape about to kill it instantly.

I also remember my Uncle Damián, Mum's youngest brother, in those years. He was a rake-thin teenager, who still embodied the hardiness of the farming men, and amazed us one time by lifting his own mother with one arm and one of our aunts with the other while they laughed, yelling at him to put them down lest they all fall and break something.

He would arrive at three or four in the morning from a disco—his being the Bonney M-, Village People-, Bee-Gees-generation—and one late night, he roused Grandma, with a loud whisper of "*¡Madre!*" outside the kitchen door, dramatic enough to awake us too.

It was a rabbit or a hare, fresh from the road, where beast and vehicle had crossed paths. Roadkill, yes. But, not carrion; he'd done the deed himself, flicking on the high beams to dazzle the animal, as it dashed across the road. The little creature would leap high, then freeze like the proverbial deer in headlights. *Ave que vuela, a la cazuela*—bird on the wing, makes the pot sing.

Supper? Not quite yet. Grandma introduced me to the realities of food and where it comes from. It didn't turn me into a vegetarian any more than it did the local people, who'd always prized the odd bit of game and survived winters on pigs fattened in the back patio, killed and salt-dried or turned into *jamón serrano*, chorizos, and so forth.

The following morning, after breakfast, I held the rabbit up by the hind legs—by the shins, I suppose. It's funny to think that a rabbit's foot lucky, considering where it came from.

The skin comes off, leaving a viscous layer underneath, which glistens in the light. I am aware of a distinct smell, unclean, nauseating, but continue to hold the rabbit firmly. This is serious business. I can't take my eyes off it, as Grandma uses her knife to neatly separate the carcass from the skin. I remembered hearing that a man would do his rounds through the village to collect rabbit pelts to make fur coats—the cheap sort that people always joked about. But this was no joke. It was, in a way, a solemn moment. Deprived of its fur, the rabbit now seemed pitifully reduced.

Grandma must have read my mind because she looked at me with her shrewd gaze, and quietly observed: "Poor little thing, right? But one must eat…"

Initiations

I spent the most memorable part of December 31, 1979—the night the world said farewell to the seventies and embraced outsized shoulder pads and even bigger hair—behind the floor-length skirts of a round table of the kind that had a thick central leg that forked out into a four-clawed base.

We were at the house of our old family friends with whom my brother and I spent almost every weekend, frequently going there on Friday evening and staying overnight to be joined the following day by Mum and Dad. It was a large family with several children—some around our age, others a few years older. The parents were each ten years older than our own, just as their eldest daughter was ten years older than I.

That New Year's Eve, as several dozen people filled up every room in the house, the patio, the kitchen and the front steps—friends, cousins and neighbors standing or sitting everywhere—the youngest member of the family, a few months younger than I and a year older than my brother, introduced us to the game of "The- Little-She-Cat." She purred and stretched languorously, as we caressed her arms and legs and back—just not too close to her ears, which elicited a growl, but soft, lest adults looked under the table. We were engrossed, curious about each other's bodies, in a way that made the act of play a façade for something terribly serious. Such was the reckless urgency of three kids aged six, seven and *almost* eight, playing this game of *La gatita* in the lounge-room of a crowded house while people talked, ate, drank and laughed all around them. The prospect of its ending with the cries of outraged parents added to the sense of trepidation; for there was nothing more than a tablecloth to conceal us.

Afterwards, taking advantage of a moment when there were no toes pointing in our direction, we emerged from our secret nest, soon to exchange kisses and good wishes with everyone for the new decade about to commence. And so, we left behind the only one that we three had ever known—the 1970s—too young to realize just how special or momentous it had been.

From then on, my own preoccupation with the opposite sex became more and more pronounced. It was about a year and a half later that Ramón and I found the Holy Grail: two girls in our class who seemed to be as curious about the male anatomy as we were about theirs. Like most adventurers on such a quest, we'd learn that *finding* the grail, though an achievement in itself, is not the same as being allowed to *take* the thing. Our failure was all Ramón's fault, of course.

Maribel and Yolanda—yes, one of the Yolandas, after all those years of mooning after them from afar—*really* were going to introduce us to the world of heavy petting, a foreplay of not-so-pure expectation. With what patience we stuck to our lesson… How our caresses travelled the tortuous path upwards from white-socked *feet*; ankles and calves, massaged—and nothing else—for the length of the afternoon; taking our leaves with ardent rectitude till the next day, holding hands, making sheep's eyes at each other; dreaming about the lifting of the hem of a skirt. Our own boyish anatomy— the baring of it—was comparatively unproblematic, and, in the end, did not even appear to be of much interest to Yolanda and Maribel. It was dispensed with after a couple of peeks and a wrinkled nose or two (*ughhh…*). Oddly, the real object, for all four of us appeared to be how much they wanted to show us, how long they could keep us wrapped around their little pinkies.

Then, during an afternoon that promised us the prize, as we worked through the layers between us and the thing itself, when Yolanda's tight exercise trunks were to give way to underpants for me to feel through, and Maribel was promising Ramón the same, *if* he promised to be gentle, he suddenly sprang forward, incisors clenched over his bottom lip. Roughly pulling upwards on Maribel's skirt, he yanked down shorts and cotton underwear together to clap his hand between her legs in a desperate grope, as abrupt and wild as it was fleeting. Outlawed for the first murder, the boy bolted headlong from our hiding-place on the side of the playground, like Judas with the purse in one hand and the noose in the other. Some years later, I witnessed the same furtive burst of aggression replicated by a bag-snatcher.

Of course, I saw the writing on the wall. I had to try. But, the girls, committed to the sharing of fortunes, good or bad, had made joint plans. Besides, they were somewhat rattled by Ramón. I pleaded and protested. I was as different; I'd be as gentle *as a lamb*. I was a S.N.A.G. before the term even existed—and possibly about as sincere and disinterested as that lot, hiding behind a façade of political correctness. I commiserated. I condemned Ramón's unconscionable conduct. In fact, I could think of nothing else, myself; and, beneath my smooth-tale, of course, I was consumed with desire, and outraged that he had so *casually* thrown away heavenly bliss for a quick snatch at joy. I pleaded in vain.

They must have noticed the lust in my eyes, and suspected the wiles of the fairytale wolf. Behind my soft-spoken words, my pleas for special consideration, they sensed a willful desire, sublimated though it was with all the cunning a nine-year old could master. Besides, their resolve was made stronger after Maribel raised the issue with her mother that night and got a good talking-to and firm instructions never to let a boy touch her again.

"But that's *just them*, right?" I asked Yolanda. "*We* are still okay, *right?*" Actually, no. I should forget it, too. There'd be no more of that. It took a great deal of effort on my part not to weep, there and then. That evening, I played with my food, a faraway look in my eyes.

Story Time

One day, Dad told us about a boy he knew at school—a great soccer player, apparently good enough to have played professionally, had it not been for deafness so bad that the referee threw away his whistle and settled for gesticulating in front of the boy to catch his attention. The shocking part was that the boy had lost his hearing due to a teacher's overzealous attempt to smack some sense into him. A burst eardrum had cost him the hearing in one ear while a subsequent infection, not dealt with adequately, had also caused him to lose the hearing in his other ear, leaving him the ten-year old deaf as a post.

Beating children was something that many in our parents' generation had grown up with. Their own parents would do it at home—firstly, because it had been done to them, so they believed that it was the proper way to punish rudeness or laziness—or to deal with any and all transgressions—and life was hard. By the same means, parents were known to expressly instruct teachers not to hesitate to beat their child if need be: "*¡Usted, peguelé si hace falta! ¿Eh, Señor maestro? ¡Ya sabe!*"

As if he were your own son, they might have added.

Let it be said that teachers apparently did not to require much encouragement for the time-honored practice. As a well-known saying sometimes attributed to the Jesuits put it: "*La letra con sangre entra.*" The letter enters with blood? Would this refer to writing? The Law? It's probably not misguided to read it as a variation on that other great religious commonplace: "Spare the rod and spoil the child."

Dad had reached adulthood with his own hearing intact, but did have a scar on his forehead, a path to his own childhood, which caused me to prick up my ears when I heard that Grandma herself had been responsible. She'd gone on an errand, and left him in the house with an express warning not to look for birds' nests on the roof while she was out. However, no sooner had she left than Dad was standing on the roof overlooking the house's inner courtyard. When Grandma returned, sooner than expected, unheard by her disobedient son, she made her way to the back of the house—eight-inch door-key in-hand.

"Luis!" she called up from the courtyard.

"*Sí, Madre,*" Dad hastens towards her side of the roof, and, reading urgency in her tone, he peeps down. The key clocks him right on the forehead, causing him to plummet onto the cobbled patio.

There is blood aplenty, and Grandma, contrite now, laments her actions: "What have I done to you, *hijo mío?* What have I done?"

"Quit it with all that '*hijo mio*' stuff! Why did you have to do it, at all?"

Hearing this tale, Luis and I burst out into the shocked, nervous laughter of disbelief. "*¡Qué bestía!*" I can't help saying. "What an animal."

"Hey!" Dad exclaims, frowning darkly. "That's your grandmother you're talking about!"

We knew of hardship and trauma in Dad's own family, too, like the disappearance of his mother's younger sister, a mere girl of eighteen and a republican *miliciana*—a female soldier—of whom nothing was ever known by the end of the war, and whose fate remained a source of grief to my grandmother to the end of her life.

But, some of the interesting stories were also told by one of Dad's oldest friends. It was with his daughters that my brother and I played every weekend. Even when he wasn't telling the story, it might be an anecdote *about* him, so that we were able to piece together the scattered fragments into the narrative of his life.

He came from a very large family and had grown up in bitter destitution. Born ten years before our own father, the Civil War still raging, he had firsthand experience of the worst years of the *posguerra*. To make matters worse, he'd lost his father during those years.

We heard of a family of nine children—fatherless, and their mother, too, only recently restored to them following a stint in political prison. They'd work alongside each other, picking through the dirt and pebbles for lentils left behind by the reapers. They would also look for damaged olives scattered on the ground, or for the few left on the trees.

He spoke with a survivor's uneasy mingling of bitterness, relief, and even simple disbelief—which gave way to hearty laughter, as he painted for us a picture of a child of five, running wild, practically in rags, but hanging off the underside of a nanny-goat to feed at her udders. We laughed heartily at the picture of this little *pícaro*, biting his own piece out of a hard, unforgiving world.

I certainly wouldn't go anywhere near a goat given my experience of these stubborn, often vengeful, beasts, an attitude that I had acquired the previous year in Mum's village after being butted and chased by a mean, curly-horned billy goat, which my cousins and I had caught, *in flagrante delicto*, ruining my uncle's veggie patch in capricious search of the daintiest leaves.

This man's father had been one of those who ended up as a resistance fighter, a *maqui*, with a price on their heads. He'd lost his life in the early '40s when the Second World War was raging, and the *maquis* still had hopes of overturning the fascist government and of restoring the Republic.

A bricklayer by trade, this man took to the hills after he was tipped off that a pair of leather-tricorned, Civil Guards were scouring the neighborhood for him. Eventually tracked down to a cave, he was shot, a state broadsheet celebrating the heroic deed of the security forces. Our father's friend had been in an orphanage when an older child showed him the newspaper. His voice rose with indignation when he described that, as he wept, newspaper in hand, an inquisitive nun backhanded him for weeping for such a man.

* * *

Even at the age of seven or so, we were not exactly unaware that he, like many in the Spanish Left, had a lot of animosity towards the clergy. We had heard of the Church's complicity with Franco's side—echoed, in fact, outside Spain, too, when the Pope himself saluted the Franco's victory as a Catholic triumph—but we also knew of anticlerical excesses on the Republican side because they were also true, and were a source of shame and conflict that was equally impossible to refute or justify.

Religion, both in terms of ideology and in its institutional role, had certainly been among the core divisive issues and sources of rancor, and for some individuals, a personal conflict. But, it is one thing to read or to hear of issues in a general way, even if balanced and considered, and quite another to have the direct testimony of an individual's personal experience.

There is context, moderation, nuance within any side, any community, of individuals. But, in terms of conflict, history will be not merely colored, but even outlined if not established by those actions and individuals that a particular community is willing to countenance, excuse or tolerate *within its own side*. Conflicting accounts seem to demand balance and reconciliation—or indifference, or impatience—depending on one's character or morals. But they may also demand continued commitment. Ultimately, some differences and conflicts are irreconcilable. One's attachment to values one deems *self-evident* or *universal* is not up to debate. Of course, the bonds of friendship, of kith and kin, and of experience and memory, also forge one's sense of community.

For me, however, it came to be about values, and *faith* of a certain kind, that would make me choose what to believe and who I might want to be. Such belief started early. And it remains at my core to this day, despite many seasons and experiences. In love and in outrage, this source of certainty was founded on an awareness that there are stories so vividly, astonishingly clear and real, that they demanded allegiance, and which go beyond the personal—even if learned from one's elders.

The quintessential story of the Civil War, for me—and it is, of course, from a time even before my own father's birth, but which connects me to him in an indelible way, as knowing it made sufficient impression on him that he was compelled to pass it onto me—concerned not any feat of martial bravery, or endurance, or of a particular act of violence—though there were certainly many of those—but of the display and expression of a particular form of power and belief that could only be abhorrent and demanded eternal defiance and corresponding opposition.

The context was the fascist seizure of Salamanca. When Franco rose up in July 1936, he headed the forces of the Spanish legion in Morocco, but soon, large areas of Spain fell, or joined forces, with his advance, though republican resistance in the larger cities meant that the war would drag on for three years. So it was that by October 12— Columbus Day—still in the early stages of the war, Salamanca— home to Spain's oldest and most renowned university—had already been taken, and would, in fact, function as the fascists' general headquarters for the remainder of the three-year war.

It may already seem a perversely ironic choice, though it may be argued that conservatism and cultural tradition need not necessarily be opposed. But the target, truly appears to have been education and freedom of thought. Among the intellectual casualties of that year was the Rector of the University of Salamanca, Miguel de Unamuno—a classical scholar and philosopher, noted for his uncompromisingly liberal and independent views, someone who had, for example, publicly condemned Republican anticlericalism, among other things.

However, on that occasion, he denounced the undisguisedly anti-liberal, even inherently anti-Christian, aims and brutality of the fascist uprising. He noted the ascendancy of specifically colonialist-military forces which were regaining prominence in Spanish affairs, and stated how such anti-liberalism and intolerance had manifested themselves in the past, in notorious acts of oppression in the late-colonial, nineteenth-century period, for which he cited the notorious execution of the Philippine liberal intellectual, José Rizal, in 1896, by then, a martyred hero of his nation's struggle for self-determination.

This provoked the ire of one of Franco's warlords, Gen. José Millán-Astray—in fact, a veteran of the Philippine War—who, thus, uttered his outlandish response: "¡Abajo la inteligencia! ¡Viva la muerte!" (Down with the intellect! Long live Death!) Soon removed from his post as university rector, and subsequently placed under house arrest, Unamuno would, in fact, be dead within weeks, on December 31, 1936.

The story, both for its basis on historical fact, and for its compelling narrative, made a profound impression on me. Ever since I first heard it, uniforms and uniformed ways—real or metaphorical, and of whatever shade or ideology—have elicited from me, a sense of distrust, along with a belief that knowledge and the principles of intellectual and creative freedom, are worth defending against the inhumane, stunting and mendacious tendencies of privilege and power.

* * *

The first time we heard that our Dad's friend had been in prison, it was inexplicable for us. Had we heard right? We were young enough not to know already, but old enough to ask discreetly afterwards, whispering to Mum to explain what that hardworking family man, Dad's best friend, was supposed to have done, and how his wife could mention it in such a matter-of-fact way.

"It was a long time ago," Mum said vaguely; and with the almost resentful lack of interest that she usually brought to the subject, she added that "it was something to do with politics."

Dad was more forthcoming. We were living in a democracy, now, after all. So, we learned that it had all happened late in the regime, during the late 1960s—when people were arrested by the *Brigada Político-Social*, notorious for their use of torture to extract information. But, even in the early '70s when my brother and I were born, though things had started to become more relaxed, people were still forbidden to participate in political rallies, or to criticize the government, or to be caught with what the authorities labeled "subversive material." His friend's political activism had resulted in his imprisonment as a *suversivo* following a mass-arrest in 1968, which had taken him away from his wife and, by then, three of their five children. Our father, though younger, had taken similar risks years later, too, but, never arrested, though he had once been warned that he was on a list of suspects, he had not faced the worst that such dissidence could incur.

This kind of thing was mind-boggling. Sheltered from the ugliness of the world by the happy coincidence of the time of our births, we had started to share the common, easygoing assumptions of mainstream culture: an acceptance of the *status quo*, that what is, is right, and that the authorities can be trusted.

On television, we watched heroic cops battling perfidious criminals—much like the cowboys and Indians, and sheriffs and outlaws of the Westerns that we adapted into the playground game of *Los buenos contra los malos*: "Good Guys Versus Bad Guys", bullets pinging out of index fingers.

Now, we were being introduced to personal stories which refused to fit our innocent worldview. Policemen whose job was to torture people? Government agents who persecuted people who disagreed with them? A dictator in the recent past—and still featured on coins in circulation at the time—whose allies had been those Nazis forever outwitted and beaten in the exciting, morally reassuring, WWII-themed films we watched on television on the weekend?

Of course, it would take a lot more to even commence my education. Back then, Spain was not exactly an international melting-pot, aside from the tourists, and, for lack of recent immigrants, Gypsies—though the Roma people have been in Spain since the fifteenth century—were always marginalized; indeed, they still face prejudice and vilification in many parts of Europe even today. Some regional minorities came next, attributed a range of stereotypical traits, and made the object of jokes, which often included parody of their accents. It is no coincidence that Mr. Jinx—the rodent-hating, braggart cat forever in pursuit of the mice, Pixie and Dixie, in the popular Hanna Barbera cartoon show—had his voice dubbed in a broad Andalusian accent, and, in fact, was known in Spain as *el gato andaluz.*

In my case, the first time I met a boy of another race, I was probably seven, but had already seen enough TV to have unquestioningly acquired all manner of assumptions and prejudices. When Dad saw me swing around with a toy revolver and cry out "*¡Alto, o disparo!*" (Stop, or I'll shoot!"), and identify myself as an Agent of the F.B.I., he simply looked a little embarrassed—mostly *for me*, but also for himself, perhaps, as he proceeded to observe to our hosts, a little flustered: "And *we*, who didn't want to have any toy weapons in the house, so the kids wouldn't develop a love for them!"

However, within five minutes, in Tobi's bedroom, his skin was all the excuse I needed to push him into the role of the black guys from the cop shows. When he retreated under the bed, I chased him and prodded his side with a broomstick, his yells bringing in all of the adults. My parents were aghast, while I, only then, awoke to the fact that this child was as human, as afraid and as undeserving of all that, as I would have been in his shoes.

The Carob Tree

"This one will hardly feel like a mosquito bite," the pretty nurse assures me, and she is as good as her word. It's the sixth or seventh injection that I've received, masked faces and rubber-gloved hands of all sizes taking turns to approach my gurney.

This I remember as if it were yesterday: Dad has taken twenty-two minutes to drive the thirty kilometers between the plot of land our friends have bought near Lliria and La Fé Hospital in Valencia, first by raising a dust cloud, as we bounced along a country lane, then, speeding along a four-lane road while Mum shook a handkerchief out of the window to alert other motorists that we had an emergency. "They probably imagined that you were about to give birth!" Dad would joke later. Highway police on motorcycles even escorted us for the last couple of miles!

For the almost ten years that I'd been in this world, aside from the common cold, a bout of chicken pox, and that sort of thing, I had not needed much by way of medical attention. I suffered a superficial cut on my right leg the year before. Since it happened in the country, and on a Sunday when the doctor in my mother's village had been away, it was stapled without anesthesia by the local *practicante*, while I gritted my teeth and said nothing, both to reassure Mum, who was holding my hand, and to give my cousins outside the door nothing to tease me about later.

But, I had never needed medical treatment again until this time.

The nurse—called Nuria, as I'd fondly recall for years—her kind face and the way she squeezed my shoulder becoming part of how I'd begin to dream of women soon after—stayed with me, telling me that I was brave and that I mustn't worry, as I was led along a labyrinthine path to the operating theatre. It's good to be a kid.

The truth is that, given my track record of taking to my heels at the first threat of a fight, I certainly wasn't particularly brave or tough. But, as I'd realize years later, medical professionals often have the ability to maintain a positive perspective which is reassuring for the patient. I also imagine now that a flood of endorphins made me feel oddly detached from the whole thing.

In a weird way, it all happened because of my lack of interest in soccer. To clarify, while my brother and our friends played soccer that Sunday—after a lunch of paella in the Valencian countryside—I was in my habitual, Sunday-afternoon spot, high up on the fork of an ancient carob tree.

Overlooking the improvised playing field, which couldn't be called dusty on account of the jagged rocks, which concealed a plague of scorpions, I'd sit, reading a book with my feet stretched out in front of me. That day, needing to pee, I tried to clamber down my usual way, swinging from the bough I was on, in order to grip one of the lower branches, and so to the ground. This time, however, I lost my grip and slid roughly down the tree-trunk—rotten through, with stake-like splinters sticking out of it. Though I reached the bottom on my own two feet, the inside of my left calf was torn to the bone.

Initially, I thought it was just a bad scratch, and I took two steps towards the half-built house where the parents were having coffee after lunch. Only then, did I realize what had happened when I looked down at a leg that was numb and would not support me. I found myself looking at this leg as if it wasn't mine. I saw Luis and our friends approach me, like shadows in my peripheral vision, and their voices sounded hollow and distant. In fact, I was puzzled that it didn't actually hurt, but simply had gone numb and on me. It should be more painful when it stung badly simply to fall and scrape your knee in the playground.

On the car-ride to the hospital, I told everyone not to worry, insisting that it didn't hurt. I told my mother not to worry about a thing while she stared at me, wide-eyed. It hurt more the next day, though, after the stitches were put in, and it had a chance to cool down. The hospital experience, though, was an eye-opener for me. To see people who attended on a daily basis to emergencies which were rare in anyone else's life seemed amazing.

During the week or so that I stayed home from school, I read a lot and mused about life and destiny. Reversing my betrayal of a couple of years back, I decided that doctors and nurses far outshone pilots and flight attendants, mere waitresses of the skies.

Dad's Study

I t wasn't very often that I went into Dad's study, his home-office and retreat. *El despacho* was where he kept his stuff: paperwork— piles and piles of it, a funny seal at the top of each page. There were also a couple of paintings, done on canvas but full of cracks, paint peeling away. It made the humble fishing boats look even more fragile—sad how things get old.

Of course, there were lots of books, too. More than my own collection, though mine was certainly growing, as Dad was sure to bring something new every few days. Some of my books had originally been stacked neatly on a bookshelf, but another lot now rose in a pile on top of the wardrobe.

I saw a small, red-handled knife on Dad's desk while he went through his account books, a look of concentration on his face. It was quite hot, as it often gets in Valencia in the summertime, and the door was wide open. Stepping closer, I tentatively picked up the knife while Dad nodded with a gesture that said, *let me get to the end of the sum…*

The blade wasn't long, but looked very sharp. It was sitting next to a pile of papers and open mail. No crumpled envelopes, gum-wrappers or notepaper, as you may find on my own desk. Unlike me, Dad has always been neat and organized and put anything like that in the wastepaper basket on the floor.

Making conversation, I ask Dad if this thing is what they call a letter-opener.

He looks at me, a slight smirk belying his pretended seriousness. "No!" he says, and suddenly adds, in a buccaneer's growl: "It's a gut-opener!" At this, he thrusts his face toward me, a grin on his face, and two hands out, curling like claws. I gasp before joining him in shared laughter.

I noticed a couple of books that I'd never seen him read. They were side-by-side on the shelf, and I wondered about them. One had gold lettering on a hard, leathery cover. It was called *The Mother*, and it was by someone called Máximo Gorki, an unusual name, I thought, thinking of one of my favorite cartoon characters. I also wondered if *La madre* dealt with the same stuff as Mum's beloved one on *Puericultura*—a very big word, and all about taking care of babies.

Right next to it, sat the other one: The Bible, which I'd long wondered about since Dad often made remarks about priests and the Church. But, of course, when I said something mocking about *beatos*—using the nickname for fervent churchgoers—Dad looked serious, and told me very firmly that I was not to say things like that, which would offend people. They had a right to their faith.

"But, what if that's how I feel? I thought we could say what we believe?"

"You can believe things. But you cannot insult people. Your rights end where theirs begin."

A little later, I asked Mum. Wasn't Dad an atheist? She almost looked stung.

"No. Don't say that! He believes in God—he even read the whole Bible," she responded. "The whole thing…"

"Really?" I shot back, surprised.

"Yes, he wanted to find out for himself. Actually, he says that if Jesus were in the world today he'd have to be a socialist—*por lo menos*…." Yes, at the very least.

I'm all ears, as Mum continues: "But, as usual, it's the ones in power who are the problem."

"*Los gobernantes…*", she trails off with a sigh.

I thought that sounded interesting. I couldn't wait to throw that one in Marcelino's face! Mum watched those wheels turn inside my head. She's always known me better than I know myself.

"And another thing, *Iván*: don't you go talking about all this stuff at school. In this life, there are things that are said at home, and other things that one says outside."

"Yes, Mum." I though a little about that, though I still felt a bit confused.

At the Seaside

Growing up, we spent little time with Dad's side of the family. Now and then, we'd visit the largish provincial town where he was born. But, unlike our month-long stays in Mum's village every summer, and shorter trips there throughout the year, we'd rarely see our paternal grandparents for more than a few days at a time, and, even then, it was usually they who came to Valencia.

Similarly, we very rarely saw uncles, aunts and cousins on Dad's side of the family, in part because they were spread out, unlike Mum's people, who all lived in a village where everybody knew them, and where even Luis and I were known by name by more people than we could hope to remember.

One year, however, we travelled down the coast from Valencia to Santa Pola, a seaside town near Alicante, where, finally yielding to repeated requests from my aunt, Dad's younger sister, Mum agreed. Aged eight and six, we spent three weeks there, mostly at the beach with our three cousins—all boys, after whom, our aunt and uncle had quit trying for a girl.

It was there that I first used a snorkeling mask. Though not particularly graceful in the water, I could swim like a dog and float like a log, which is all that was needed to peer down through the calm Mediterranean waters at the tiny fish darting around the algae, or to catch hermit crabs. We spent entire days doing little else before we moved onto the next obsession.

The place was a fashionable seaside town of the kind that flourishes in the summertime but is not so charming or sought-after the rest of the year—though, like Valencia to the north, it was blessed with glorious weather.

These were our rich relatives, as our aunt had married a successful engineer from a well-heeled family. We heard of visits to fashionable restaurants, and of outings to the opera or to the theatre with well-connected acquaintances. But their eyes grew large when we asked for a full glass of milk, and our cousins, then, insisted on the same thing. When our parents came to pick us up at the end of the month, our uncle joked that, seeing how my brother and I ate, the following year he would rather buy us a suit.

My memories of those three weeks include a visit to Santa Bárbara Castle, Alicante's Gothic cliff-top citadel—which, many years later, I'd rediscover as the setting of *The Changeling*, one of my favorite Jacobean tragedies.

It's interesting to consider the things that one recalls or fails to retain. I remember some children at the beach, small rippling waves, row after row, and the clear blue sky, infinitely far. There the dying sun sinks in an orange glow, inspiring the children to fantasize about an ocean of Fanta! I couldn't help thinking about how the sand would really stick to you then.

We spent our days at the beach, building enough sandcastles to match the ruins which dot the lands of Castile and Aragon. Then, after getting there soon after sunup and having to be dragged out of the water in the evening when our teeth chattered and our lips turned blue—at night, we sat in the apartment's terrace, which overlooked an open-air cinema. That's how we saw *Jaws 2*, that huge mouthful of teeth coming at us like a nightmare and probably about as wide as our own mouths. It was certainly a great choice of film to watch in a place somewhat similar to Amity.

That may have been the night I wet the bed. My uncle wondered how I had managed to empty my entire bladder. The mattress was soaked right through. But if dreams of sharks had anything to do with that, it didn't stop me from getting in the sea the next day.

The beach was practically downstairs from my uncle and aunt's place—just a couple of minutes on foot. So, we were left by ourselves. Grandma came at some point—one of those times when she came on her own, typically leaving Grandad behind in the country, or sending him off somewhere else. Family lore has it that she sent grandpa to my parents' place, shortly after my brother's birth while she hastened to join her own pregnant daughter.

Initially, my uncle, or my aunt—even grandma—would stay with us at the beach. But, later, since we knew our way and were so close to the house, we were only fetched if we failed to go upstairs by dinnertime. As the eldest, at the grand age of eight, I was in charge of my brother and our three cousins, who were seven, six and five. Everything is new and wondrous when you're only eight—or seven or six....

So, we cut across a park and went to the shops to check out the latest rage: the *Comecocos*—A.K.A. *Pac-Man*. But, best of all, not far away, we discovered a disused worksite—what was left of a rock quarry and, beyond it, the trench-traversed site of an abandoned building project.

There, we play war-games, hide and seek; we have target practice, throwing rocks at stacked empties, and while the sun beats down on our backs, our minds focused, we strain, using hands and feet to clamber up and down the steep incline. We progress to a perpendicular rock-face, easily rising the height of three apartment floors. We keep this up almost the length of the afternoon, returning to the beach for a final dip before going upstairs to have dinner, saying nothing of our adventure. None of us let a word slip—not even the youngest, still five.

One day, however, we are told to return by 3:30 because we need to go somewhere. We are supposed to meet Grandma near the beach, but we are not there on time. We, who just a week or so earlier had floated face-down at the seaside for hours, marveling at little fish, and had thought and spoken of nothing else, are now consumed with our latest pursuit, climbing. We chase each other up and down a steep slope, or strive to reach the top. We are proud of the little things that we are learning along the way: how long we can hang by our fingertips; how much we can count on rubber-soled beach sandals and canvas sneakers; when to rest and breathe between footholds. The sun still beats upon us because if Alicante is known for one thing, apart from its palm-lined avenues, it is for its long, dry summers.

Suddenly, the sun is gone, its brightness outlining some overarching buildings and hillocks while we, in the shade, occupy a lunar landscape in the shadows. God! It just comes to me. It must be hours since I even thought of the time. We were supposed to meet Grandma at three-thirty? Four o'clock?

As I look down, I feel my head swim, a sinking feeling in the pit of my stomach. We quickly dust ourselves down. Even Luis, still six, looks terribly serious, as we head back, sprinting for the pedestrian crossing, across a road and under some kind of rotary overpass that we think of as a giant Scalestrix set.

When we arrive, panting, at the front of the building, we see our rather pissed-off uncle, probably biting his nails for a couple of hours, a cigarette in one hand and an empty packet crumpled in the other.

"May one know where in the Devil you lot got yourselves into?" He asks. But he doesn't wait for an answer:

"I thought you could be trusted, Ivan. You *are* the eldest, *¡ostia!*" He swears by the Host. He sometimes does so, casually, but rarely in anger. He is, by nature, mild-mannered, apart from the odd, muttered aside—even a bit unassertive, taking all the kids out of the house whenever my aunt, or his mother-in-law—or *both*—get into a bad mood, which is often. If we are ever a bit rude, he asks, a smirk on his face, if we'd like *"una galleta de cinco dedos"*, a five-fingered biscuit. The very idea makes us laugh, but we behave anyway, just in case someone else gives us one.

This time, though, he is obviously upset. I start to tell him that we hadn't been far, but he cuts me off. Our grandmother had been about to go to the police station to report us missing. We'll be lucky if she doesn't give us a good belting, and we shouldn't expect him to stand in her way. He starts to say something else, but stops abruptly, points at the stairwell and yells: "Upstairs, the lot of you!" As we file past, heads low, contrite masks for faces, butt-cheeks a little clenched, he calls out over his shoulder: "Tell your aunt that I'm off to the *estanco* for cigarettes."

I couldn't help but remember the story about the man who told his wife just that and wasn't heard of again for a long, long time until he returned, an old man, tired of life in the Americas. I wonder, even today, if my uncle himself ever thought about that story.

The Swing

O n the upswing, it takes all my concentration to keep from going into orbit, or to keep the seat of my pants in some semblance of contact with the seat of the swing, and stop myself from going beyond that point where I imagine I would vault all the way around. On the return, I feel her hand on my lower back, attuned to the tempo of it, knowing the moment when this human pendulum will start to swing forward again, and adding to the momentum of it all.

I am flying: a nine-year-old astronaut, swinging back and forth, my feet stretched out before me, impossibly far into the sky; while, coming back, feet curling back beneath the seat, I touch her elbow for a bare instant. She is thirteen and different from her sisters and from any girl I've ever known. There is her off-the-wall humor, her gift for telling ghost stories that make us pee our pants.

She's a little high-strung, perhaps, her tantrums are legendary—like the time when she refused to wear clothes for a week, and her whole family ended up having to let her be until she got over it. She is an irrepressible, indomitable wild-child, though her older brother knows just how to get under her skin, and he can drive her completely nuts.

She was a source of fascination, of course, and the object of a real crush—an impossible love, which she returned with a big sister's fierce affection.

The rhythm seems to be increasing, and, yet, it is as if everything outside of me were standing still; the same treetops, ducks in a pond, the same people in the distance, frozen in mid-step, as if caught on high-speed film; the noise of traffic in the road just beyond; children in the park all around me; the cheers, yelling and laughter. All of these are dulled, dimmed, now, a reassuring, lulling hum in my ear; I am no longer attuned to it, like when I read and people have to shake my shoulder to get my attention. Only now and then does a snatch of conversation reach me, entering the portals of my mind; detached, disembodied words float there.

"Maybe you shouldn't push him so hard...?" the tentative question drifts in the air.

"Nothing's going to *happen* to him", she replies; and she adds: "He's *loving* it"—which happens to be the truth.

She still has the accent that she acquired during the year that she spent with relatives down south, in Seville. No-one can make a roomful of people burst into laughter like her, or take the breath right out of your mouth; the things that she will sometimes say—things girls never used to say—women mutter and cluck their tongues.

That habit of hers has been known to work to our advantage, though.

Not long before, when we were staying in her house—my brother and I played with the two younger sisters—some of their friends had come around to play: two girls and another boy, whom we teased, saying that he was the boyfriend of one of the girls. Then, we ensconced ourselves in one of the bedrooms to play "*Beso, verdad y atrevimiento*", something like "Truth or Dare" if you will, but nothing like the stuff we were gossiping about that day. The neighborhood rumor mill was preoccupied with what some of the teenagers had been getting up to in a nearby building scheduled for demolition.

Though we had an ear to the door, wary of approaching footsteps, the house being full, we were caught with our pants down—at least, I was, *literally*—fully exposed, in response to a dare, the darer now looking more embarrassed than I was, even before her older sister—the girl pushing me on the swing—barged in, and burst into laughter, pointing, as I, naturally, swung towards the door: "*Pero... ¡Los muy sinvergüenzas!*" (Yes, shameless brats—that was *us*).

"I knew you lot had to be up to *something* when I saw this door closed and not a peep coming out!"

My jaw drops, and it's not the only thing hanging. She tells me that I should zip up now. Then, just as suddenly, she's slammed the door on her way out and she's gone like a passing hurricane.

Immediately, above the hum and drone of adults in Sunday-afternoon conversation—voices fueled by coffee and cigarettes, brandy, and the eternal subject of politics—we hear her exclaim: "Would you believe those little *microbios*? They're all *fucking* in there!"

A roar of laughter exploded from the lungs of the thirty-seven people, crowded, standing-room-only, in the lounge. Luckily, this was the extent of the reaction to what she had just said was going on behind that bedroom door. Oh, and her mother, added: "Oh, that girl of mine! What am I going to do with her? Tch, tch, tch! What things she says!"

Back in the air, still flying, I daydream about those times when we sit together, the TV off, or no longer noticed; on the sofa, legs stretched along its length, reclining, her back resting against my chest, or I in her embrace, warm blanket around us, I caress her long arms lazily with the feather-light touch of my fingertips, our breathing slowing down; her eyelids, I can guess, get heavier and heavier, until, at last, I feel her arm grow limp, her breathing deeper, and she is in peaceful slumber.

Eyes closed, I can feel us, her warmth, the silky skin of her arm, my fingers moving softly; for such little effort is needed to caress someone. I must be dreaming, asleep in mid-swing before I realize I'm flying for real, now, through the air. I hear a shriek of "*¡Que se me* *mata!*" But, I won't die. I see treetops, the stretch of sand and grass coming faster towards me, as I hit the sand, turning head over heel, limply like a rag-doll. I rise again, before she and her friend can reach me. On unsteady feet, the drowsy, numb smile of one gently woken from a pleasant dream, I say, that I'm alright. They dust me down, fuss over me; she insists on carrying me in her arms, part of the way back to the house. But I walk again, later, eating an ice-cream, my hair tussled playfully, as we cross the threshold.

Other Places, Different Times.

When we heard stories about our grandparents' younger years—or of our own parents' childhoods, for that matter—we would be shocked, and not a little grateful to have been spared the hardships of the very different world in which they had been born. But often, these stories were also curiously exhilarating, even funny. Some of them concerned childhood pranks or some memorable event or other.

I remember being approached by a middle-aged woman, as I waited my turn at the butcher's—an errand from Grandma. My mother, apparently, had been a very bad child. I've sometimes wondered if she, or others like her, actually expected me to change the way I looked upon my own mother. In a way, I did, but not as they probably had hoped. I did learn about some of the events and the culture that had shaped her.

One of these accusers showed me a small scar on her forearm, which I later asked Mum about later. She frowned for a moment, and then, suddenly understanding, she laughed till tears ran out of her eyes. "Are you telling me that this *tonta del pijo* (dickhead) is still crying about that?" She asked, shaking her head, an ironic smile playing on her lips. "So, she showed you the *watch* I gave her, huh?"

"A *watch?*" I ask, puzzled.

Mum simply grins and brings her teeth together in a firm, theatrical bite.

"You did *not!*" I explode with laughter. "But, *why?* Why would you do such a thing?"

As it turned out, Mum, only nine or ten at the time, had been a bit of a brat. She and her friends would tease the local teenage girls out on their Sunday walks with boyfriends. Perhaps, it was when they threw burrs at the back of their *mantillas*, as they passed, which, back then, could have caused a teenage girl an uncomfortable scene at home.

Three of these older girls—the woman with the *watch* among them—had ganged up on my mother, pinned her down in the dirt of a country lane and pushed a dead bird into her mouth.

A few days later, my mother, sitting at her doorstep, narrowed her eyes when one of the older girls literally skirted along the wall across the street to avoid her.

"This is precisely what ticked me off. I was going to let it drop. But when I saw her act like that—all prissy and stupid—I ran her down. And, well…. there, she still has her watch!"

The other two girls avoided her street altogether. But, after that first fight, it was too late for them. Mum waited for them near their houses, and, once she had caught them on their own, neither age nor size kept them from being thrashed by the pint-sized berserker. Nobody ever messed with her again. But, of course, one day when I visit the village again, it's possible that some elderly woman may pull me aside and shake her walking stick at me, in remembrance of what a fierce creature my Mum was at the age of nine.

These word-of-mouth stories told among family and friends, were far more interesting than the daily melodramatic radio-plays to which the older people still listened, rapt, during the scorching-hot siesta hour when we kids were sent to bed for our own good, or, having evaded mothers, aunts and grandmothers, ran ourselves ragged in the streets or in fallow fields. I remember approaching some people, absorbed over a radio-set, out in the porch. I heard the high-strung, plaintive voice: "*¡Coge mi navaja y matame!*" (Take my pocketknife and kill me!) Yet, the real people we knew had lived lives no less fraught with drama, passion and suffering.

Seeing that paved streets, running water and toilets only transformed Mum's ancient village in 1980—when I was eight—it is hardly surprising that my parents and grandparents grew up in a world that was not substantially different from what it might have been in the nineteenth century.

My maternal grandfather learnt to drive after his retirement. Then, he drove a Dyane 6, just like Dad. But, only a few years before, he had still been ploughing his fields with a pair of mules, useful beasts of burden which also made it possible for him to cart melons and other produce to neighboring villages. He started to work when he was seven or eight, which had continued to be the norm for many years to come. My own father started at twelve, although the simple bad fortune of his mother's year-long internment for tuberculosis had also played a role in his premature removal from school—doubly sad since he had been a diligent student who had risen three grades above his own age group.

Those times were hard, indeed, both during and for many years after the war. When my maternal grandfather returned to his hometown from Valencia—the seat of the Republican government during Franco's three-year siege of Madrid—he had lost his older brother, killed in the battlefield. Their younger brother, known to have served in a combat battalion—and, therefore, deemed to have "blood on his hands"—had wisely crossed the Pyrenees. There, in Lyons, the young man had settled down with a French wife and raised a family. Only decades later would he visit the village again, the two brothers embracing, once more, after so many years. My mother and my uncles and aunts, in turn, had also met two cousins—by then, almost grown men—whose family resemblance was patent in the old photograph I was shown, but with whom they had been unable to have a proper conversation.

In the early postwar years—while World War II wound to an end, and the hopes of the resistance fighters and other defeated republicans to be liberated by the Allies were dashed—Grandad also saw his older sister soon sent to prison for eighteen years for harboring *maquis*, along with her husband, who received an even longer sentence of twenty-five years. Millions of tourists were already flooding into Spain to the sinister slogan of "*España es diferente*" before that poor man, broken down by a quarter of a century of forced labor and brutal treatment, was released from prison.

I don't remember meeting him, though I heard of his death as something recent when I was very young, and I do remember visiting the home of my great-aunt, and the family of cats that she raised in her own final years. It was to their home in Valencia that my mother, still in her mid-teens, had initially gone when she left the village to seek domestic work as a nanny in the city.

Grandad's three small vineyards were the fruit of backbreaking work carried out in some of the darkest years of the century—the years of famine, as they were typically called. He acquired them by working through the winter months when there was hardly any work, and even most of the poor resigned themselves to sitting by the hearth. He was soon joined by his eldest sons, who cleared the snow and dug the frozen ground beside him. They cleared rocks, stumps and roots from the old orchards and hunting grounds of rich landowners, who paid my grandfather a portion of the land rendered fit for the plow.

The family also survived on the outlawed barter that had always gone on among peasants. At a nearby bakery, my grandfather traded for flour the very roots and stumps that he and my uncles had pulled out of the ground and hewed to pieces using wedges and sledgehammers. He did so, that is, when their cart wasn't intercepted by members of the local garrison of the civil guard, who staked out country lanes to seize the firewood or the bread for their own families.

But worse yet had been the early years when my eldest uncles—war babies—were still children. While the country still reeled from the losses of the battlefield, the firing squad, prison and exile, the haphazard abuse of the local authorities was aggravated by more systematic gathering of supplies for the armies of the Third Reich—for, thus, Franco honored his debt to his allies.

Family lore includes the tale of how my maternal grandmother outwitted the Civil Guards, who had learned that she had a large sack of flour, the family's winter store. Shelling peas with a toddler on a blanket in the front patio before the portals, she heard the approach of the *pareja*—the dreaded pair of guards in their boots and patent-leather headgear.

The thick wooden bar served as a kind of bolt was in place, but they still could reach in and physically lift it to push the gate open. She heard them fumble for it, urging each other on even as she climbed to the top of the great wooden door, balanced herself with difficulty, and knelt on that wooden crossbar.

The men strained, as they envisaged looting her home, and she heard one of them say: "A wily bitch she is—this one! She's sure to be in there, and she's supposed to have a great, big sack of flour. *¡Coño!* This feels like it's nailed into place... Ugghh!"

Grandma turned her head to look at her firstborn son, whose mouth, a first tooth showing, she had kept open with a stick—to protect his eardrums—during a night of bombing, in Valencia, near the end of the war. Now, she gazed into his eyes, a mere few feet away on his blanket. She pleaded inwardly: "Don't you cry now, *rico*. Not now!"

"*Más listo que el hambre*," she chuckled when she recalled—by then an old woman reminiscing about times long past, a tear in her eye and bittersweet joy in her heart. My uncle had been "smarter than hunger"—not one peep out of his little mouth, like a clever little leveret, dead-still on a clump of dirt. It had been as if he'd understood that life depended on it. When the uniformed men returned later, there had been nothing for them to find.

Grandad's last years of work, in turn, were hard because after years of combining seasonal work on large estates with his own small crops, he had to work full-time as a field-hand to qualify for the old-age pension—calculated on the last years' contributions. It wasn't that he was in poor physical shape—the fact that he went on to live for another three decades, is a good indication of his natural vigor. The trouble was that his teeth were in poor shape, and meal-breaks were hurried, boot-camp affairs around a common pot, a thick slice of crusty country bread in-hand. The men would have to get back to work before he'd even had a chance to eat, so he was hungry till nightfall.

I remember being five and a half—the precise time when Grandad turned sixty-five—and the day that he weighed and measured me at the farmer's co-op. I weighed twenty kilos and was one-twenty in height. He also showed me his new teeth, which he was clearly enthusiastic about. He had every right to be: those dentures probably meant the difference between a long life and the prospect of a swift decline into ill-health.

But, I also remember one my aunts, who exclaimed in disgust when she saw her father-in-law's new teeth: "Ugh! How can you bear to put those things in your mouth? The Lord knows where those teeth came from! For all you know, they got them from dogs— or from the dead!"

Grandad couldn't help but laugh at the backwardness of someone who was, on top of everything, so much younger than he. Many were the times when he'd shake his head at things like that. Many years later—the last time I saw him, when he was in his mid-eighties—he told me: "I've often marveled at her. She's perfectly capable and sharp in so many other ways—don't get me wrong— but, sometimes, you'd think she was raised up in the hills, in a cave!"

*　*　*

My own father left his hometown at fifteen to find work in Valencia. The day Dad first left his provincial hometown in La Mancha, his father, sporting the traditional beret and old-fashioned suit he wore for the rest of his life, accompanied him part of the way to the train station. As they reached a bridge which Dad was to cross alone, his father, fiddling with his pocket watch, told him two things: that he himself would never leave his *pueblo* while he had a hunk of bread to eat, and that my father would be crying before he reached the other end of the bridge.

In one version of this tale, Dad, his pride stung, didn't write home for months, though he himself, realizing the effrontery, revealed that, in fact, after a few days at the home of grandmother's cousin, he had been reminded of how much they awaited news from him back in the countryside. This I credit, given his old-fashioned duty where his parents were concerned.

When Dad's older brother also moved to Valencia, the two young men—still in their teens, in fact—worked at the same factory, making shaving brushes.

A year or so later, after my grandparents and my aunt, Dad's younger sister, had joined them, they left Valencia for Toulouse. But Dad's older brother, already enrolled and shortly to commence his compulsory term of military service, had to remain behind, though he, in his turn, rejoined the family in France almost three years later.

During those years, my father learned a proper trade— construction, for which there was great demand at the time. But, first, he and grandfather spent the first year in France as *terrassiers*, digging foundations with a crew of other immigrants, most of them *Maghrebi* people from the then-newly-independent nations of Morocco, Tunisia and Algeria. Ironically, while those immigrants sought work in France, there were many of their former colonial masters, the *Pied-Noirs*, who still rankled at what they perceived as the French government's betrayal, in granting those nations their independence—enough so, that a significant number chose to start new lives in Francoist Spain rather than in democratic France.

After a year as a laborer, my father, eager to learn the builder's trade, requested training to earn third-degree qualifications as a starting point. He found the opportunity with another company, and worked his way through third and second ranks, before finally obtaining his full trade certificate. He, then, returned to Spain for military service with an offer from the company to renew his employment with them upon completion. That would be in 1968.

Two years after that, his roundabout journey led him back to Valencia, where my parents' paths finally crossed, and, in the spring of 1971—almost 50 years ago, as I write this—they were married.

*   *   *

One of my favorite memories is of summer nights in my mother's village when people sat on chairs outside their front portals and talked to the neighbors across a narrow, unpaved street, long into the night. There, having played all afternoon with our cousins, only stopping for a *merienda* of cheese and ham or sardines, inside a gargantuan piece bread, and back out for more games of hide-and-seek or some form of childish mayhem till light and our legs finally gave out, we would eat a late dinner and then sit outside with our grandparents.

The lady from the house across the narrow street told of her brother's close call with a snake which had curled up inside a basket at harvest-time—thick as a rope, and longer than a fryer-full of *churros*, she said I shuddered, as I remembered the story I had that my father's own great-grandfather had been crushed in the coils of a similar specimen—found by the well to which the old man had gone to draw water.

These long nightly conversations would end sometime past midnight when Grandad, straightening up and seeming to feel the air with face and nostrils, would remark gravely: "*Es hora de irnos. Ya parece que viene la maréa.*" The *tide*, as he called the cool, damp breeze which would immediately become apparent, was, indeed, a desert chill, so, gathering our chairs, cups and other things, we would retire for the night.

Stories would be revisited and asked about in later years. I might ask Mum about some puzzling thing I recalled, and she'd fill me in, her face momentarily brightening, as she recalled it. There was the story of Grandad, who hurt himself during one of the harvests when a strong man in his prime stood to make a lot of extra money. A huge load that he'd been trying to secure on his cart gave way, and, though he had narrowly escaped being crushed, he found himself alone, on the side of a field, staring at his left leg, the knee dislocated. But, there had been nothing else to do but grit his teeth, take the limb in his own two hands and push it back into place before the swelling made it impossible.

Back in the village that night, Grandma and one of her neighbors worked on that knee, rubbing it with alcohol and one of those herbal preparations in which some women of her generation were still skilled. He may have limped for a little for a day or two, but he had not missed a day of work that harvest.

Not surprisingly, as a child, I saw him as larger than life: tough, yet gentle with a good, kind heart. So he seemed in a story of human meanness and suffering of the kind you hear in small communities. The events had taken place when my mother was a very little girl— sometime in the mid-1950s—and it concerned a young bride whom Mum saw only once or twice. Little more than a girl, obviously sickly and fearful, she was a neighboring farmhand's wife, her health failing. To make matters worse, she faced the added trials of having a brutish husband and a prying, malicious mother-in-law. Mean-spirited and tightfisted in the extreme, mother and son denied the young woman sufficient food to eat while any perceived transgression on her part resulted in a beating. When it came down to it, it might have been simply that she had grown too weak to work and was resented as a burden. If the mother-in-law sniffed out that she was cooking some meat for herself, she would rail that the young woman was squandering her son's earnings. The young woman might have answered back, or was deemed disrespectful, in some way. In any case, her husband would be informed when he returned from the fields, and a beating would follow, the thick wooden staff of his hoe his preferred instrument when disciplining a slip of a girl who was swiftly succumbing to consumption.

Neighbors became aware of what was going on. But, though an extreme case, even for times when domestic violence was not exactly unheard of, it was not the authorities' custom to intervene in a married man's domestic affairs, nor for other people to involve themselves in problems outside their own family circle.

Grandad went as far as anyone ever did. On one of his short journeys to the young woman's village, he spoke to her family. But, even they did nothing to take her home, leaving it up to my grandfather to deliver her to them on his cart.

When she met him at the threshold, he had to physically carry her to the cart—not hard, since she weighed no more than a girl of twelve, Grandad recollected, leaning on his walking stick, tears in his eyes, some forty years after the events. He pointed out the house with a jab of his chin to indicate where it had all unfolded. There, mother and son had peeked out through the curtains. My grandfather told me that he paused briefly that day, staring back at the window, his hand clenched around his own staff.

"He didn't come out, though, that son-of-a-bitch", Grandad added, his eyes filled with pity and renewed indignation. "His mother must have known that it wouldn't be as easy as thrashing that *chiquilla*."

Sadly, though, there wasn't much to be done for that young woman, who died only days later, in her parents' home. Grandad clucked his tongue, shook his head sadly, and gestured for us to proceed on one of the daily walks on which I joined him that spring when I last visited the village, in 1997.

The Heart

I t was around the middle of 1980 that Dad gave us a big scare—the summer when he turned thirty-five, quite a few years younger than I am now. The stresses of a busy life, fueled by innumerable cups of black coffee, work and nightly political meetings must have taken their toll.

Back from work, he was taking us on the weekly shopping trip. Luis and I, in the back of the car, prattled, bickered and fidgeted, as usual—intermittently told to hush back there because they couldn't think, or talk or drive. Except, that is, when we did the television commercial for the latest panty liner: *It doesn't show! It doesn't move...*

That afternoon, the flowers are in bloom on the hedges alongside the road. Reeds line the irrigation ditches of the *huerta*, and the fields are green with market vegetables. The sun, in afternoon descent, casts a veil of orange over everything. But, in front, Mum and Dad are tense. She keeps on asking Dad what's wrong. He denies that there's anything wrong, and I feel like she is nagging him. But, she insists, saying that something is happening, something is wrong: "*Sí. Te pasa algo. No me digas que no....*"

We are suddenly very quiet, all ears. I feel my own heart beat under my ribs. Then, the car veers brusquely to the side, and Luis and I rise off our seat. There's only the seatbelts holding us back, the sight of the *huerta*, and ditch-rushes swerving to meet us while Mum's voice rises, high-pitched: "*Pero, ¿qué haces?*"

Dad has pulled over and hit the brakes, the dust still settling around us. Stunned, we watch him burst into tears—something I don't think I'd ever seen him do before—as he immediately tells Mum that he's been sick.

It all comes out. At lunchtime that day, he had lost his balance. Suddenly out of breath, as the ground spun around him, he had collapsed in the street. A passersby half-carried him into a nearby pharmacy. The attentions of a concerned pharmacist were all that he needed for the time being. But he'd also been to see a doctor that afternoon.

It was his heart. One of those warnings that may or not be taken seriously, but had better be. A year earlier, when my parents had travelled to the Soviet Union, a medical checkup had turned up a minor sign of heart trouble, which Dad had not followed up on. It's hard to consider changing your lifestyle when you're thirty-something, have other concerns on your mind and feel pretty much indestructible.

But, this morning, it had been different, and with that strange tendency for life to flash before one's eyes, it had brought into focus many things that had been bothering him in the quiet hours. It may have been the technocrats, who were shouldering aside the grass-roots militants while growing dissent replaced the common ground formerly shared by activists opposed to a living dictator. Ironically, the unity of the party's outlaw years—the subject of militant stories about *la clandestinidad*—suffered its worst test when the party finally became a new player in the fledgling democracy of the transition years.

Back from one of his adrenaline-pumped *mitins*—political *meetings*, as I'd realize years later when I'd learned English—he'd often be agitated, upset. I distinctly remember the pain he'd bring home. It was in the late '70s and early '80s that the party, following the trend elsewhere in Western Europe, shifted to embrace

Eurocommunism. However, it failed to prevent, and may even have hastened, the party's fragmentation, the expulsion of the secretary general after a quarter of a century at the helm, and the loss of its once considerable popular following, so that today, the party has less than a tenth of the more than 200,000 card-carrying militants that it boasted in 1977, the year when it was legalized.

I remember the time when some disagreement about policy ended with someone taunting him. Still fuming when he got home, he told Mum about it, and I heard Mum gasp: "You shouldn't say things like that!"

I was all ears. The other man had told him: "Oh, I thought that you were Pro-Soviet..." I wanted to ask what it meant to be *Pro-Soviet*. Weren't *all* Communists "Pro-Soviet" of necessity?

My father proceeds with his telling: "So, he backed down and told me: 'I'm sorry. I was only joking!' And I told him again: 'I shit on all your dead!'"

Mum shakes her head. "I don't like that kind of thing—not at all."

There's another anecdote that's stuck in mind. Mum told me of my father arriving home disgusted by an offer to work professionally for the Party. He had been offered a post within its bureaucracy. "*¡Liberaté!* Come and work for us", he had been urged. But, despite the risks that he had taken for his ideals under the old regime, and though he continued to devote his time, attending meetings—and even donated his services as an accountant—he refused to become a party employee, someone who would draw pay and who might—as he scornfully put it—claim the cost of a new tie as a business expense.

In the course of that year, Dad moved away from organizational and administrative roles, remaining just another supporter while he sensed—quite rightly, as it turned out—that the Party's glory days were over. It could be said that, in more ways than one, his heart was simply no longer in it.

Nineteen-Eighty-One

This one was a crucial, momentous year for the fate of the entire nation, never mind one nine-year-old.

On the very day of my birthday, the twenty-ninth of January, as we prepared to cut the cake, an exultant neighbor knocked on the door to tell us to turn on our television set. There, the icing on the cake, we watched Adolfo Suárez, head of the conservative government, resign live on national television! The smiles of our parents, equal parts joy and disbelief, were mirrored in our childish faces, no doubt. Of course, celebrations were not on the level of the day in late 1975 when, legend has it, the nation's supply of sparkling wine was exhausted in response to another news item, no *cava*-cork left unpopped.

The following three or four weeks were momentous, at least from where I stood. I started to pay more attention when the television was switched on. I would listen avidly to news reports on the radio in our kitchen; I would read newspapers and magazines on the weekend. Some of the stories continued to play around in my head for days and weeks—even years—to come.

The mother of a little boy spoke to the press after her child was mangled by a terrorist bomb. Spared death, he had suffered severe burns, and had also lost an eye, two of his limbs and the means of ever fathering children. Attempting to make sense of the situation, the five-year old's mother attached blame to everyone and everything. Though she condemned the people who left the bomb in a box at the supermarket to do its indiscriminate harm, she also felt that the store management should have removed the box. She even meekly suggested that her young boy had been partly at fault for kicking the box.

I was puzzled and couldn't let it go. So, I read that passage to my parents, who were sitting in the lounge room. My mother was aghast; *the poor child* was *not to blame!*

"He didn't do any wrong, the poor little angel", she added.

Angelitos, I learned, were a common commodity the world over, in places that I was only hearing about for the first time. More weekend reading—perhaps the same publication—told me the tale of another child, also hurt by those who should have known better. A third-world boy, eyes dark and deep, stared out of the page of the illustrated text.

Handsome as he was—the journalist went on—*that one could envisage how his gaze would soon have had girls sighing for him, he'd been rendered pure as an angel, an example of practices among certain cults in that remote nation.*

"You are pure, now!" ecstatic devotees had reportedly exclaimed in praise of the boy, as his severed genitals were ceremoniously wrapped in silk. I read on in disbelief, and, for days, I talked of little else to friends, teachers and family.

In the meantime, events continued to unfold closer to home. Catching a few minutes of the news, one afternoon, I saw a policeman who openly, even defiantly, admitted to having fatally tortured a member of *ETA*—one of the extremists from the Basque Country, who were campaigning for independence through terrorist means. Some said that terrorists like that had it coming, and that he couldn't very well expect fair treatment—children, thus, voiced their parents' opinion in the playground. Others remarked that the Basque people—even radicals who planted bombs or shot people—had been justified to fight back in former times when the police would arrest them and beat them merely for using their own language in public. But, with Franco dead and a democracy in place, *what could they want, now?*

In times past, many people had, indeed, sympathized even with the outlawed terrorist group, for example, when they outwitted the security services of the dictatorship to assassinate Franco's right-hand man—his *dauphin*, Carrero Blanco—who was blown onto a rooftop, three-ton limousine and all, in 1973. Growing up, I heard a joke, which I was told was current within hours of Franco's death of gangrene in 1975:

> *Carrero Blanco meets Franco at the Pearly Gates. He reproaches the Generalissimo: "You have taken your time to join me!"*
>
> *"What did you expect?" replies Franco. "All of us don't get to come by car."*

I couldn't help thinking about the little boy in the supermarket, though.

"*El que a hierro mata, a hierro muere*", Marcelino utters sententiously: "He who lives by the sword, dies by the sword."

The terrorist in question had been tortured at Carabanchel Prison, in Madrid, in a building where the security agent interviewed on television, or others like him, had tortured the so-called subversives of the pro-democracy struggle not many years before. Without batting an eyelid, the policeman explained that he had burnt the soles of the man's feet. Whatever else he had done—I cannot recall if the unrepentant agent went into further detail—the prisoner had left the premises feet-first.

Amidst the debate, conflict so deeply rooted, so hard to unravel that even the children argued about it in the playground, an interim government struggled to keep afloat in the early weeks of February. This went on until something happened to confront and frighten all but the youngest: *El golpe*, the failed coup-d'état of the 23rd of February, 1981, in which two-hundred submachine-gun-wielding *guardias civiles*, led by Lieutenant-Colonel Antonio Tejero, burst into the Congress of Deputies. It was on the day when the appointment of a new president, Leopoldo Calvo-Sotelo, was to be formalized, and a date that I'm not likely to forget.

Mum picks us up from school, visibly nervous. Holding hands, we walk quickly through the *huerta*. She tells us that she will explain later. It is obviously grim news; we are afraid to ask.

It is over the very next day, but the night is long and tense. Dad doesn't come home that night. Mum has been told that he's alright but needs to lie low and wait it out. I imagine that whoever else had been at that last meeting with him did likewise—that they didn't risk crossing a city suddenly, even improbably, plunged into *estado de excepción*—state of emergency—a curfew imposed by the local military authorities, but which, evidently, did not apply to the right-wing militiamen already in the streets, vowing to root out all the Reds. If the coup turned out to be successful, men like my father were going to be hunted down. Mum is up half that night, tip-toeing from her bedroom to the bathroom.

Whereas proceedings were broadcast live on the radio, national television studios had been seized. Most of the images everyone would later see only emerged when it was all over—the television footage that a RTVE cameraman had the guts to continue to record for almost half an hour in the house of representatives, and then switched with an unexposed roll under his captors' noses. This was emitted till it was etched into the collective memories of a nation.

Lt. Col. Tejero—quasi-Napoleonic in his uniform—waved his gun around and shot at the ceiling, ordering everyone to get down on the floor: "*¡Al suelo todo el mundo!*" Other paramilitary Civil Guards seized control of the chamber, firing guns in the air. A reporter for the state radio station explained that they would have to cut their live broadcast, and added the detail that their captors were armed with submachine-guns.

While most hit the floor, the defiant few who refused to do as ordered must not be forgotten. They were the still-acting president, Adolfo Suárez, a gun to his face and somewhat roughed up; the Minister of Defense, General Gutiérrez Mellado, who ordered Tejero and the others—all, in legal fact, his subordinates—to stand down; and, lastly, there was Santiago Carrillo, General Secretary of Spain's Communist Party—a man then only recently back from decades in exile—who proceeded to light a cigarette. As his predecessor, Dolores Ibarruri, dubbed *La pasionaria*, had famously uttered a lifetime before with words redolent both of Republican defiance and Spanish anticlericalism, *Más vale morir de pie que vivir de rodillas:* "better to die on your feet than to live on your knees."

Years later, Carrillo would explain that he had understood immediately that until the coup was successful those men would not dare to shoot anyone; and if they had been successful, he would have been the first to face the firing squad.

So, Tejero had his day: gun in hand, his fascist arrogance of a piece with his outsize moustache and his shiny leather hat—the aptly named *tricornio*—to complete the portrait of a man committing an act of sacrilege in a place of civilian government.

The hat was also the ideal thing to conceal the horns of a cuckold, which the Spanish proverb says "is always the last to know." This man did not understand that Spain was no longer his *madre patria*. Rejuvenated, and neither modest maiden nor dutiful wife, Spain had reinvented herself overnight, finally emancipated.

Things return to normal son, and it is then, that we hear that Tejero and his Civil Guards in Madrid had surrendered without bloodshed—and so too, in our own hometown, the military which had deployed 2,000 soldiers and fifty tanks into the streets to seize Valencia.

The statement by the King, both as Head of State and in his capacity as commander of the armed forces, is heard on the radio, and is later broadcast on national television, where he appears several hours after the start of the coup, in his military uniform.

Even on the Left, most people granted that he had acted properly, restating the legitimacy of democratic institutions at a time when many still questioned his own role as a monarch—the grandson of Alfonso XIII, whom the Second Spanish Republic had deposed in 1931. For Juan Carlos derived his status as Head of State directly from Franco, himself, who had designated him his successor in that capacity.

Perhaps, in other parts of Spain, the coup only entered reality through the public media of radio, television and the newspapers—in the domestic space of people's own homes. It was believed that the coup was to have been much bigger—a highly coordinated, nationwide conspiracy; that various generals had gotten cold feet—or perhaps simply hesitated, expecting others to go first in actually putting the bell around the cat's neck. Valencia, however, was different. When we left our apartment the day after that when it was all over, we looked at the face of our neighbor—one of those *uncles*, Dad's close friend—gazing confidently out of an election poster, and we looked upon that face with something other than a sense of quiet pride in knowing him. We were relieved for him—another man who probably didn't go home the night Dad stayed away—just as we felt relieved for ourselves and for our own father.

"*Milans del Bosch ¡Al paredón!*" demanded a sign, hastily painted on the side of a building, naming the commander of the army garrison in Valencia. "To the firing-squad." Tempers were certainly running hot, and with good reason—though, in fact, democracy would save the guilty from such a sentence, since the death penalty had now passed into history where it belonged. But, to think that a *capitán general*, entrusted with national defense, should have conspired so late in the twentieth century to do, once again, what his predecessors did two generations earlier, in 1936, by rising up against a democratic government in order to drag the country back into the nineteenth century.

Valencia had seen the seizure of its government buildings and of television and radio stations, as dozens of tanks and other armored vehicles materialized everywhere, and caterpillar chains had torn up the asphalt in our own city street.

There were always some during those early years who would utter some variation on: "Whatever we want to say, life was better under Franco." The polite thing to do and the most democratic was simply to reply: "Or *worse*."

Only in 2005, a few months before the thirtieth anniversary of the dictator's death, was a statue of Franco finally removed from its pedestal on a Madrid street, and the decision by the Socialist government of that time was still being criticized by senior members of the conservative party, then in opposition, one of whom accused then-President Zapatero of attempting "to bring the past back to life" ("*resucitar el pasado*").

I was too young to have heard half of the stories of the tough years in which my parents and my uncles and aunts were born and raised. But, feeling my mother's fear that night, much as she strove to keep her composure, was enough of a taste of what it meant to live in a system in which people were forced to live on their knees.

Silkworms

S omeone gave us some silkworms, which we kept in a shoebox and watched as they ate their way through fistfuls of mulberry leaves. Other kids said that the really cool thing was to see the silkworm spin itself into a cocoon. But, ours weren't quite there, yet.

Raising silkworms was a fad that year—kids took them to school. The cocoons weren't much to look at. The pod was about the size of a fat thumb, a dirty off-white or yellowish color. It looked a bit like a peapod, only not green.

To get the silk, people were said to boil these cocoons before the caterpillar had a chance to undergo metamorphosis and emerge through a hole, rather like a chick coming out of an egg. I mused about that. Those caterpillars would not be turning into butterflies! I had heard of people who were against fur coats and would protest outside department stores and throw abuse, as well as eggs and other stuff, at the bitchy rich ladies who strutted out in their furs. The protesters would get themselves arrested and dragged away. But, no-one was going to get too upset about some silkworms.

For days, we watched those caterpillars, as they ate their way hungrily through mulberry leaves. We'd been warned not to feed them other stuff, like leftover salad, and it seemed funny that I could eat artichokes and peas and lettuce while a bug could be so choosy.

Then, one day, we look in the box to find that one of the caterpillars has vanished, replaced by a cocoon while we weren't watching. In a few days, would we find an empty husk, a tell-tale hole in the side, and the butterfly gone?

It doesn't get to that, though. Dad enters our room with an anxious look on his face, asks where the silkworms are, and leaves hurriedly to throw them in the bushes across the street. In-and-out in thirty seconds, he didn't give us any time to protest or even to ask *why*; not only fast, but also with a certain agitation written upon his face, which immediately reminded me of the time, years earlier, when I saw him overcome his squeamishness with a gesture of disgust, as he rushed to the balcony, holding a dead rat by the tail, spring-trap still attached to its head, and he whisked the whole thing into the irrigation ditch across the street with a jerk of his arm.

When he returns, smoking, his nerves calmed by the nicotine and by the ritual ashing of the cigarette between drags, he explains that while on his rounds, he has seen a couple of houses utterly overrun with the things—worse than an ant invasion. Although that sounds unpleasant enough, even to us, who had been happy to raise a colony of the creatures in our own bedroom five minutes ago, Dad speaks to us calmly, a little later, and we understand that something far more sinister had been on his mind.

It was early May, less than three months after the momentous events of the 23rd of February, and the latest news were enough to make anyone more than a little edgy. A mysterious sickness—a syndrome—had caused the deaths of several hundred people in just two or three weeks. Hospitals in Madrid were filling up with thousands more, affected by what, for lack of a better name, had been dubbed *El síndrome de Torrejón* after the locality where the first victims had resided.

Torrejón de Ardoz, in the region of Madrid, was known as the site of one of Spain's three U.S. Air Force bases, which served to cement American recognition of the Franco regime in the mid-fifties, as the Cold War elevated the Spanish *falangistas—*

cronies of Hitler and Mussolini—into allies in the struggle against international Socialism. When Franco died in 1975, Richard Nixon, true to form, labeled the dead autocrat "a loyal friend and ally of the United States."

In 1981, the year that would also witness the grim emergence of AIDS as a modern plague, there was news of a mysterious syndrome in Spain, some kind of new disease which caused muscle spasms, severe aches and pains, hardening of the skin, renal failure and gastrointestinal damage, as well as cardiovascular problems which included blood clots. Some victims suffered lung damage, and were said to die of asphyxia.

Talk of chemical and bacteriological experiments—of the possibility that it was some kind of germ warfare, either an actual attack, or a test out of control—was commonplace. It probably didn't help that Torrejón was the site of a foreign military base. "If they have to kill us," someone said, "let them, at least, line us up and shoot us, and not give us diseases!" (Yes, *they*). "What are they trying to do to us? These bastards will end up making us all rot!"

Several weeks passed before the finger was pointed at a scam involving adulterated oil that had been sold door-to-door. Rapeseed oil—of which *canola* is a variant—previously denaturalized for industrial use, had been artificially flavored and passed off as virgin olive oil. By the time the connection was exposed, over 20,000 people had been affected, and hundreds had perished, to be followed by others who died of complications. To this day, many Spaniards still feel queasy even thinking about canola oil—much as people understand that canola oil is not toxic *per se* and is consumed widely in other places.

The reports about the role of that *aceite de colza* fraud, commencing in June 1981, did not put an end to alternative theories, however. People noted apparent inconsistencies: reports of families in which one members developed symptoms, or even died, while other members didn't get sick at all; and claims that some of those affected had not even consumed the oil. One of the most prominent dissident voices until his death of cancer three years later was none other than Dr. Antonio Muro, then-director of Madrid's *Hospital del Rey*, where the majority of patients had been cared for. Dr. Muro conjectured that the cause had been a mysterious pesticide, which rendered the plants highly toxic. Beyond questions about the precise identity of the toxic agent, some elaborate scenarios theories placed blame on a global pharmaceutical company—and alleged that the oil-fraud story allegedly a cover-up to protect its financial interests— alternatively, the U.S. military, based in that area, was alleged to have caused the problem, deliberately or accidentally, according to different scenarios, as part of some chemical-weapon development.

Some of these theories, and a range of testimony associated with them, emerged years, even decades, later. But the sense of uncertainty—of being in a precarious position, one's very health at the whim of others—was there from the start, in the spring and summer of 1981.

The Door.

D ad is on the phone, talking to the immigration officials, the tenseness in his voice unmistakable despite his well-honed phone manner. With a muttered oath, he slams the cherry-red receiver into its cradle, then sits quietly, crestfallen, his nostrils flaring as he exhales, fuming. Our friends left for Australia a year ago, and there is no news yet regarding our own application to travel to Australia, too, on a skilled-immigrant visa program.

Suddenly, he springs to his feet, and with a snort, he crosses the lounge in three leaps, towards his study, and he toe-taps the door to his study by way of opening it. The door barely swings on its hinges, and Dad finds himself with his moccasined foot grotesquely suspended in midair, like a piece of abstract art, inserted askew in a flimsy frame.

Dad's mouth hangs as much as our own, as, sheepish now, he frees his foot from the shattered remnants of the cardboard-laminate paneling. The shoe, a shell as hollow and vacant now as the dubious door, remains in its socket, a piece of abstract art, as Dad stutters something about the quality of cheap consumer products.

That same afternoon, he fixed the door, carefully stretching over the breach some adhesive vinyl in a wood-pattern. Thus, it would remain for the few months that were left us in Spain, a nagging reminder of Dad's sometimes short fuse.

Final

It is July 11, 1982, a Sunday. Tonight, Italy will defeat West Germany, 3-1, to win the FIFA World Cup. Spaniards—most men, certainly—will be glued to the screens, tuning in to the broadcast on *La Primera*, RTVE1. The other television option is the other state channel, RTVE2.

Tomorrow morning, we will pick up our suitcases, drive to the airport and fly with a plane-full of British soccer fans to London's Heathrow Airport. There, after an eight-hour wait spent watching people drink tea and eat buttered white-bread sandwiches cut into triangles—we shall board a larger plane, a Boeing 747, which will refuel in Bahrain, and again in New Delhi, on its way to our final destination: Sydney, Australia. Mid-flight, Dad will turn 37, and Mum is 33, Luis is 8, and I am 10.

We said goodbye to our relatives in the country a few days ago—our cousins crying more than us, as we waved goodbye and got in the car. Today, we had lunch with some friends, but, in the evening while Dad and Luis watch the final with our great friends next door, Mum and I stay in the house, excited about the long flight ahead—especially I, who have never been on a plane—but also a little tense about what awaits us on the other side. None of us speak any English. I was very amused the other day when told that *yes* is English for *sí*.

So, Mum and I watch the epic Soviet film broadcast on RTVE2—an epic, three-and-a-half-hour-long film called *Siberiade* (Dir. Konchalovskiy, 1979), which is being televised in Spain for the first time, and which Dad thinks should have been shown any other night but the Grand Final.

It is ironic that, out of my two parents, Mum should have been the one to watch a celebrated Soviet film which traced the lives of two Russian families—one rich, one poor—over several generations from the Tsarist period to the 1960s. Unlike my father, my mother has never been particularly committed in politics. But, then again, neither did she like soccer any more than I did.

The film was the most amazing thing that I had ever seen. Even at ten, I sense that the political message was a bit heavy-handed, in places, but this work also surpassed the particular—perhaps even the *particularities* of state-funded art—by projecting its vision onto a canvas large enough to expose the melodrama of history: the patterns, the ironic reversals and repetitions. It was beautifully photographed—shot in 70mm, as I would learn years later—and some scenes and images were so memorable that they remain edged in my mind even as I write, today, twelve years older than my own father was when we boarded the plane the next day.

There was a scene in which a taunting, well-fed girl tricked a poorer peasant boy into stripping and running naked around a well, amid the ice and snow of winter. There was also his attachment to a curious stranger, a radical fugitive, as it turned out, whom the Tsar's police soon caught up with, though not before he had made a deep impression. As he was led away, there was a bittersweet farewell, as the engaging rebel urged the boy to have hope and await the future. There was also a scene in a haystack, where a rich groom roughly tore open the bride's blouse, and her breasts spread out—like fried eggs, though I. She, then, ran away to join the man she really loved—the boy from before, now a young man. Mum said that she was a bad woman. I thought her divine, but, then again, I was ten; what did I know?

In any case, it wasn't the particulars that really mattered but the overall effect, a sense of the magnitude of history, and of the daunting task of retelling it; the necessary, unavoidable incompleteness of even—or, *precisely*—the most exhaustive attempts to be all-embracing; a canvas in which a set of brush-strokes, traced carefully with one's eyes, scratched at to reveal what lies beneath the surface, serves only to expose the unraveling threads beneath, and only leads one into a realization of a plurality of directions.

Would the film have made quite such an impression on me any other night, anytime other than on the eve of the day when our own family set off on a life-transforming journey? For that matter, what if I were to watch it *again*, years later, more experienced about life and about art, and more adept at reading and interpreting texts and films? I imagine so. How could it not? But, though I might—indeed, must—one day soon, watch *Siberiade* again, I have never gone out of my way to do so, instinctively mindful of my own memories of that evening and of the web of personal stories of a special time and of the place to which they are linked, and even of the many experiences that were to follow.

* * *

CPSIA information can be obtained
at www.ICGtesting.com
Printed in the USA
BVHW041537250321
603416BV00007B/839